NORTH COUNTRY

CONSTITUTIONAL REFLECTIONS ON NORTHUMBRIAN INDEPENDENCE

WITH A DRAFT CONSTITUTION FOR THE REPUBLIC OF NORTHUMBRIA

W. E. BULMER

First Published 2023

The author's right to be identified as author of this book under the Copyright, Designs and Patents Act 1988 has been asserted. © 2023 W. Elliot Bulmer

ISBN: 978-1-4467-4627-1

Published by
Lulu.com

CONTENTS

INTRODUCTORY ESSAY

This short essay on the constitution of an independent Republic of Northumbria is presented as a contribution to the debate on Northumbrian independence, sparked by the formation in late 2020, by Dr Philip Proudfoot, of a Northern Independence Party (NIP). There is here no attempt to resolve the basic question of whether an independent Northumbria is desirable for its own sake. Instead, the aim is merely to sketch-out a constitution for Northumbria, in the hypothetical event that such a state were to be established at some point in the not-too-distant future. What values and principles might it be founded upon? What constitutional rights, institutions and structures would give effect to those principles? How might the constitution reflect Northumbria's historical and social contexts and its economic and strategic situation?

The fact that a party proposing Northumbrian independence has been formed, and has struck a chord and attracted even a little interest, points both to the uncertainty of our times and to the contested legitimacy of the existing British state. It is a fascinating indicator of the territorial dimension to British politics that is increasingly being expressed, not only between the constituent countries of the United Kingdom, but also regionally within England.

Despite being incorporated into England for over a thousand years, 'the North' has maintained elements of its own identity, which are now becoming politically salient. Without falling into clichés and cloth-cap stereotypes, it is fair to say that there remains a deep-rooted and longstanding Northern distinctiveness. This is evident not only in terms of folk culture, dialect, climate, topography and cuisine, but also, compared to England's richer south-eastern core, by a different political culture arising from different experiences of both industrialisation and deindustrialisation.

The North's coal, steel, mills and shipyards, as well as its engineers, inventors and scientists, provided much of the economic backbone of the British Empire, but the North has also borne much of the cost of economic change since the 1980s. Neo-liberal economic policies, begun under Margaret Thatcher and continued with vengeance under the guise of the austerity imposed by David Cameron and his successors, have exacerbated inequality, poverty and precarity throughout the United Kingdom. The North of England has, however, been affected disproportionately – and, unlike Wales and Scotland, has lacked the institutions to soften the blow.

There is therefore an undeniable geographical dimension to poverty, and a regionally differentiated experience of austerity. This is reflected in much lower levels of public infrastructure spending *per capita* in the North compared to London. The North-South divide has widened, while the Government has proved itself to be incapable of keeping its promises of 'levelling up' in public spending or of devolution of real powers to 'Northern powerhouse' city-regions.

These different historical experiences have given rise to different social and political values, whether expressed through the liberal 'non-conformist social conscience' of the 19th century radicals, the Working Men's Clubs and the Labour and Co-operative movement of the 20th century, or today's politics of an economically, culturally and politically peripheral North defined against a metropolitan South.

Strong regional authorities, enjoying substantial autonomy under a written constitution for the United Kingdom, or even better an independent England, might be a sufficient solution to this problem. Such regional authorities would disperse political power and thereby help to achieve a better geographic distribution of public spending, economic activity and life opportunities. Perhaps most Northerners would be satisfied with that arrangement, if it were entered into with commitment and in good faith. The North East's rejection of the devolution offered in 2005 has been interpreted by Westminster and Whitehall as a sign that the North, and England generally, has no appetite for regionalism. However, what was rejected was thin gruel, a meagre half-measure of devolution, amounting to little more than a reorganisation of local government. Genuine devolution, which would give the English regions powers at least equivalent to those of the Welsh, if not the Scottish, Parliament, has not yet been offered. To embed those powers, it would be necessary to entrench them in a new constitution – a written, supreme and fundamental law, judicially enforced, and amendable only by a special process.

That constitution could deal broadly with the institutional and territorial distribution of power, guaranteeing not only devolution, but also regional representation in a reformed Second Chamber, together with protections for fundamental rights and codification of the key conventions of parliamentary democracy. Over-centralisation is just one of a host of problems. The whole uncodified constitutional system is a mess and all of it needs fixing. It was already worn-out before Brexit.

The chaos of the period from 2016 to 2019, followed by the resurgence of majoritarian rule under Boris Johnson, has broken it. From threats to hobble the Supreme Court and the Human Rights Act to restrictions on the right of protest and the abuse of so-called 'Henry VIII powers', the Government appears to be launching a revenge attack against all institutions that it views as obstacles to unlimited executive power: Parliament, the courts, the civil service, and civil society. A political system based on unwritten rules and on the self-restraint of 'good-chaps' cannot withstand such shameless constitutional hardball. The limits of making do and muddling through have been reached. The problem is not merely that the rules are being broken; rather, we have now reached a point of such profound constitutional confusion that no-one can really be certain whether the conventional rules on which British democracy is built still exist at all. Without these moorings, the state is constitutionally adrift.

No longer is 'making it up as we go along and calling it flexible' an adequate response to this crisis. In the wake of Brexit and Covid-19, key constitutional questions have been torn open for the first time since the end of the Jacobite wars: Who are we? What do we stand for? What will we not stand for? How should we govern ourselves? How will we hold those who govern to account? How can we fix a state that seems mired in incompetence, corruption and cynicism? How do we build a country where all our children can live in decency and dignity?

It would not be difficult, as a technical exercise, to devise a constitution for the United Kingdom – or an independent England – that would provide credible and compelling answers to these questions. The problem lies in the apparent unwillingness, or rather inability, of the existing state to engage in such fundamental renovation.

The constitution has, moreover, reached a point of disintegration and disarray that can no longer be fixed by the sort of bodge-job reforms that were rushed through when Tony Blair was Prime Minister. Piecemeal tinkering has run its course, and any further attempts to patch it up will only add to the general sense of chaos, crisis and incoherence. To fix the constitution would require a proper constitution-building process, but the insurmountable, existential, difficulty for the current constitutional order is that any constitutional reform process big enough to fix it is also big enough to break it apart. The existing state cannot continue as it is. It cannot dare to reform itself. It is tragically stuck.

In this context it is not difficult to see why some are now despairing of the possibilities for change within the United Kingdom, and look to independence instead. The Tories' persistent, apparently failure-proof electoral dominance in southern England only adds to the sense of futility. After decades of being ignored, patronized, marginalized and misunderstood, some Northerners, like many Scots before them, might reasonably conclude that devolution is 'a long wait for not much', and might see independence as a better and bolder, if not exactly easier, option.

Although this frustration and impatience are understandable, Northumbrian independence remains, for many good political, practical, economic, cultural and institutional reasons, an improbably remote proposition. Politically, it will face a long uphill struggle. Plaid Cymru and the Scottish National Party made their first electoral break-throughs in the 1960s, and it has been a long road; although devolution for Wales and Scotland have been achieved, and independence is perhaps closer now than ever, the United Kingdom remains stubbornly intact.

The NIP's pitch of an independent Northumbria has not yet been tested with the voters. Only time will tell whether the NIP will gather enough sustained support to enter the political mainstream, and then make a credible push for independence. If they can reach that position, it is likely they can only do so through the intermediate aim of devolution. Recognising this reality, it is probable that Northumbrian independence is not intended, even by its declared supporters, to be an entirely serious proposal. The most credible interpretation is that the NIP's pro-independence rhetoric is mainly an exercise in political hyperbole, designed to draw attention to the North's needs and to push for major devolution, at least as the first stage.

Yet, even if Northumbrian independence is not intended an entirely serious proposal, there might be merit in taking it seriously as an intellectual exercise. It provides us with an opportunity to think through, in detail and in practical terms, what would be involved.

From a state-building perspective, Northumbrian independence would be a hard task. The contrast with the situation north of the Tweed is notable. Scotland has almost all necessary component institutions of statehood: Parliament, Government, courts and a legal system, its own auditor-general and ombudsman, and civil service offices in Edinburgh delivering considerable policy-generation and implementation capacity. It lacks only its own armed forces and diplomatic and consular services. Constituting an independent Scotland is mostly of matter of putting a constitutional foundation beneath, existing, working, widely accepted institutions. Northumbria, not having the experience of devolution to build upon, is in a much less favourable position. Apart from some cash-strapped local councils, Northumbria has no political institutions of its own. They would all have to be created.

It is not only a matter of state institutions. The difference in civil society is stark too. Scotland has its own pressure groups, professional associations, national religious and cultural bodies, all the warp-and-weft of a flourishing civic life. Except for a few branch offices in Manchester, Northumbria has none of that.

Economic and fiscal difficulties of Northumbrian independence must also be considered. All northern regions currently depend on fiscal transfers from London and the South East. Independence would provide an opportunity to reconfigure the economy, to develop industries, to invest in infrastructure, and to unlock the North's great – but in recent decades squandered – economic potential. Indeed, the chance to bring about that change would be one of the main benefits, if handled well, of independence. But even in the most optimistic analysis, that is a medium-to-long term prospect. In the short term, an independent Northumbria might be even poorer that it already is, especially as it would have to fund all the institutional running costs of statehood.

This reality is in itself, of course, an indictment of the over-centralisation of English governance: that it leaves North denuded of civic, social and cultural, as well as political, autonomy, and it has weakened the northern economy to the point where it is dependent upon hand-outs from London. The conditions that make a northern renaissance necessary also make it difficult to achieve.

Then there is the problem of identity. Some NIP supporters might have gone so far as to suggest that 'Northumbria is not England', asserting Northumbrian-ness as a *national identity* with its origins in the Anglo-

Saxon kingdom of Northumbria. However, this remains a minority view. Most would-be Northumbrian citizens have a Northern *regional identity*, which sits alongside complex and contested, but enduring, English or British identities. In many cases, people do not necessarily connect most strongly with the North as a whole; they might identify primarily as 'Geordies', 'Liverpudlians' or 'Mancunians', for example, and then as either English or British, with their Northern identity squeezed between the two. Even the precise borders of 'Northumbria' are yet to be determined. Some suggest that Northumbria should be coterminous with the arch-episcopal Province of York, while others propose using the NUTS1 statistical regions (the former European Parliament constituencies) of the North West, the North East, and Yorkshire and the Humber. Many of the symbols of modern nationhood – a flag, anthem, recognised capital city – simply do not exist, or only exist in contested form. An independent Northumbria, if it were ever to come about, would have to do a lot of nation-building, as well as state-building.

None of these difficulties – real and severe though they are – is necessarily a clinching argument against Northumbrian independence. However, independence will not do much good unless the Northumbrian state actually *works*. If the basic premise is that an independent Northumbrian state will do a better job of serving the people, managing the public realm, and promoting the common good, than the United Kingdom has done, it is not enough merely to break away; it is necessary to build better, constituting an effective, inclusive and legitimate Northumbrian state that is able to turn public demand – for growth, infrastructure, more opportunities, better public services – into achievable outcomes.

The constitution – as the basis of the political and legal order of the state – is therefore absolutely central to any discussion of Northumbrian independence. It cannot be ignored. It makes no sense to talk about the policies that a future Northumbrian Government might pursue, unless there is first an agreed, workable mechanism for choosing a Government, selecting and implementing policies, and holding that Government to account.

Get the constitution right at the outset and good things might come from it. Get the constitution wrong, and an independent Northumbria might join the list of other independent states whose first hopes were dashed by falling into dictatorship, oligarchy, anarchy, or other forms of misrule.

The NIP, when first launched, indicated support for a modern written constitution, although at the time of writing no mention of it could be found on their website. If that commitment to a written constitution remains, it is a good start. Independence – a mere change in flags and boundaries – is never an end in itself; it is valuable mainly because it provides a chance to re-make the institutions of the state, and to establish them on a more democratic, inclusive, public-serving basis. The best case to be made for Northumbrian independence is that creating a new state would provide an opportunity to achieve all the longed-for democratic reforms that seem impossible in a British context. Northumbria would not be burdened by the hubris and delusions of an aged post-imperial state; it would not be worn down by the weight of tradition; it would not be strangled by the Old Etonian ruling class.

Even if an independent Northumbria is not a likely prospect in the immediate future, drafting a constitution for such a state is therefore a useful exercise, because it acts as an imaginative window through which we can look beyond the current crisis to envision alternative and better constitutional futures.

Besides, there is no harm in a bit of contingency planning. If an independent Northumbria were to emerge (and stranger things have happened), it would remain the neighbour, and presumably be the closest trading partner and staunchest ally, of the other parts of what are now the United Kingdom: Scotland to the north, and rump-England to the south. Families would continue to stretch across both borders, cultural links would be maintained, and no doubt there would be a need for a series of treaties – on trade, freedom of movement, reciprocal rights of residence, military and consular co-operation – that would of necessity recreate many of the formal links between them. It is therefore in the interests of everyone to ensure that an independent Northumbria, if it were to exist, would be a stable, peaceful, democratic and successful country. No one wants to live in a failed state, nor to have a failed state next door.

These two opposing considerations – openness to the possibility of improvement and recognition of the risks of failure – should together bound our approach to the constitution of an independent Northumbria. A constitution can make things better, but above all it must help prevent things from getting worse. Both of these considerations point to the advantage of drawing largely upon the experience of those countries that transitioned from British rule to independence in the middle decades of the twentieth century, as well as upon more recent cases of constitution-making in the Commonwealth.

This Commonwealth focus reflects the fact that constitutions are not just the products of momentary artifice; they exist, and develop, in certain historical, institutional traditions. There is a 'Westminster Model' constitutional tradition on which an independent Northumbrian state would be wise to build. This tradition extends back to Magna Carta. It encompasses such defining monuments as Petition of Right, the Habeas Corpus Act, the Bill of Rights Act, the Great Reform Act, the Parliament Acts and the Human Rights Act, as well as a body of conventional practice and a set of canonical authors – Bagehot, Dicey, Mill, Jennings and others – who have given theoretical expression to those conventional practices. It comes with a lexicon – 'vote of no confidence', 'Leader of the Opposition', 'Erskine May', 'Hansard', 'early day motion' – opaque to those outside the tradition, but instantly familiar to those who know it.

These statues, conventions, canonical authors and received lexicon together form a coherent, durable and replicable whole. Reform and renovation within that tradition – building new institutions from familiar materials and according to well-proven, tried and tested patterns – offers a surer path to success than any attempt to design new institutions in a normative vacuum.

This is not, however, a static tradition. Within it can be found examples of just about every constitutional desire on the reformers' agenda: Barbados, Malta, Trinidad & Tobago, Fiji and Dominica are all republics; New Zealand, Malta, Fiji, and many Australian states, use proportional representation. Almost all protect and reassure their citizens through written constitutions, with justiciable bills of rights, that cannot be amended by ordinary legislation. Most place limits on prerogative powers by codifying the vital conventions of parliamentary democracy – requiring the Head of State, for example, to appoint the Prime Minister based on the confidence of the elected House, and regulating matters such as dissolution of Parliament. Many seek to protect the independence and neutrality of the permanent judicial, electoral and administrative machinery of the state from political interference, by creating Judicial Service Commissions, Electoral Commissions, Public Service Commissions, and similar institutions. All these things are part of, not alien to, the British constitutional tradition as it has developed in the Commonwealth. A written constitution for an independent Northumbria might borrow freely from the diversity of this tradition, and incorporate from it many specific reforms and improvements, without risking unproven novelties.

The draft constitution presented here draws from several Westminster Model constitutions, especially but not exclusively on those that combine a unicameral Parliament with a republican head of state: Malta, Fiji, Bangladesh, Samoa and Dominica, amongst others. No one is followed slavishly, but best practices are combined and adapted. There is nothing here that would strike a comparative constitutionalist as dangerously innovative.

The constitutional amendment formula (a two-thirds majority vote in Parliament for most amendments, backed by a referendum for amendments to the most fundamental parts, such as human rights provisions and the election of Parliament) is also, although not perhaps a universal standard, a common amendment mechanism in unitary Westminster Model democracies. It is designed to make the constitution capable of change, in situations where such change is widely supported, while protecting it from easy, unilateral, destructive change.

Some provisions, however, are based on a smaller range of examples that nevertheless seem to embody specific, welcome, reforms. For example, the requirement for the Speaker to act impartially is embedded in convention and tradition in the United Kingdom, but in the constitution of a newly independent state it might be worth formally declaring, so that expectations are clear. This provision, found in section 88(3) of the draft below, is drawn from the Constitution of Tuvalu. Similarly, the Speaker's right to summon a sitting of Parliament when prorogued or adjourned (section 101(5)) – something that Speaker John Bercow long argued for, to prevent the Government from avoiding parliamentary oversight – is derived from a somewhat similar rule found in the 1970 Constitution of Fiji. Requirements for parliamentary committees to reflect the partisan balance of Parliament (section 97(4)) are inspired by similar provisions in the Constitution of Malta. The mechanism for electing the President by a two-thirds majority vote of Parliament on the proposal of a nominating committee, a method intended to ensure that the President is widely respected as a figurehead, and not too closely associated with any party, is largely borrowed from proposals articulated by advocates of republicanism in Australia in the 1990s.

Effective and enduring constitutions usually arise through an extensive political process of arguing and bargaining; they are based on cross-party agreements sustained by widespread public consent. That process – the constitutional conversation and settlement – cannot be by-passed. It does not do to predict, or pre-empt, the outcome, even for a somewhat hypothetical country like Northumbria. To reach such broad, binding and lasting agreements on the foundations of the legal-political system is not easy. It requires a well-structured process and dedicated institutions: for example, a Constituent Assembly (perhaps made up of Northumbrian MPs) in which the arguing and bargaining over the constitution can take place, a legal and technical Secretariat to support it, and a public outreach and participation programme. It helps if all this is laid down in a Constitutional Transition Act, to give the process a clear statutory form, backed by adequate funding and bound to realistic timelines.

A crucial question, which must be addressed in the Constitutional Transition Act, is what process will be needed to approve the draft constitution agreed by the Constituent Assembly: can the Constituent Assembly, by its own authority – perhaps by a two-thirds majority vote – adopt it, or must they go back to another authority – to Parliament, or to the people in a referendum – for formal approval?

This draft constitution does not prejudge the decisions of a Northumbrian Constituent Assembly. Its purpose is illustrative and instructive, not prescriptive. It places before an audience unfamiliar with, and often sceptical of, written constitutions a plausible example of a technically sound, institutionally solid, Westminster Model constitution for an independent Northumbria. It does not claim to be the final word in what a constitution for Northumbria *should* necessarily look like, only to inform and encourage public debate by showing what a viable and acceptable constitution *might* look like.

Nevertheless, we can with reasonable certainty say what sort of constitutional design choices (what combination of institutional options from the vast array of proven Westminster Model building blocks) might be suitable for Northumbria. These choices are different from those that might arise in the context of a United Kingdom, or even an independent England. In all likelihood, a United Kingdom would have to retain the monarchy, would need to be federal or at least have constitutionally embedded forms of devolution, and would have to be bicameral with a second chamber representing the territorial diversity of a large, diverse state. An independent Northumbria could have a much leaner, cleaner and simpler constitutional structure: a unitary state with a unicameral Parliament, elected by proportional representation, would be sufficient. In other words, the Northumbrian Parliament might look more like the Scottish Parliament than the Westminster Parliament.

Northumbria could also be a republic. This would be a means of asserting its own identity. An indirectly elected figurehead president would cut ribbons, bestow honours, lay wreathes, and dine with diplomats. They would have certain 'reserve powers' of a constitutional nature, but they would not have a policy-making role; for the most part, they would, like the monarch, act strictly on the advice of the Prime Minister of Northumbria.[1]

Northumbria would contain Harrogate as well as Hartlepool, and Hebden Bridge as well as Huddersfield. We must not ignore the existence of the northern middle class. Constitutions cannot be one-sided expressions of a particular party's manifesto; they must be rooted in genuine compromise, and aim to embrace the common-ground that all democrats can share. Even so, a written constitution for Northumbria could probably be bolder and more radical than any constitution that would have to accommodate the demands, culture and assumptions of southern England. There is probably a broad enough

---

[1] It is interesting to consider whether an independent Northumbria might, instead of a figurehead president, have a constitutional prince, performing a similar role. The Duke of Northumberland is an obvious candidate. Or maybe even a Prince-Bishopric under the Bishop of Durham? But here we depart from the realm of the unlikely, and enter that of the fanciful.

commitment, across Northumbria, to values of solidarity, equality, mutualism and the common good, on which to establish a Northumbrian democracy making ambitious constitutional commitments to socio-economic rights.

Above all, a Northumbrian constitution could be a powerful engine for driving economic development. The once-proud North has been starved of infrastructural and industrial investment. A good constitution would recognise the country's depressed and under-developed condition, and would establish the institutions to turn this around.

This constitutional commitment to reconstruction and reindustrialisation is not only to be found in the opening commitments of the constitution (section 1(2)), nor in the exhortations of the Directive Principles (section 42), nor even in the specific institutional machinery set up to manage economic planning and industrial policy (section 152). It is, rather, to be found as a constant theme throughout the whole constitution. The combination of parliamentary government, unicameralism, a unitary state, and proportional representation, is designed to be as inclusive as possible in the decision-making process – letting everyone have their say, including minorities – while also being rigorous, efficient and responsible in implementing decisions. A government backed by a parliamentary majority can actually govern; but it can only govern in so far as it carries the parliamentary majority with it – and that majority will not, thanks to proportional representation, be a falsely inflated one. It would not be possible for a party with 40% of the votes, under this constitution, to have sole power; it would have to bargain, compromise, form coalitions, broaden its base. That coalition, subject of course to parliamentary scrutiny, in which the Opposition parties would have a vital role, would then be able to carry out its plans, for which it would be accountable at the next election.

All the rest is merely detail. Some of those details are important. The rules for the Electoral and Boundaries Commission, the Human Rights Commission, the Public Service Commission, the Judicial Service Commission, and the Ombudsman, for example, help to maintain the integrity and impartiality of state institution, over and above party politics. That, too, is intended to support effective development: nothing spoils a state faster than a corrupt and incompetent administration, or a warped judiciary that does not uphold the rule of law.

The independence of the Auditor-General is vital, likewise, to prevent public money which should be used for development purposes being siphoned off or squandered. The rules protecting the rights of the opposition are designed to promote accountability and transparency, and to ensure that all interests are fully considered in formulating policy, so that growth and development are inclusive, and ecologically as well as financially sustainable. The rules on ethical standards in public life are designed to tackle the culture of corruption and cronyism that has wasted billions and to restore zealous norms of institutional rectitude.

The overall intent of this constitution is to enable the Northumbrian state to deliver the goods and to make a practical, tangible, material improvement in the lives of its citizens. The whole ethos of the Republic, expressed in every line of this draft constitution, is one of public service. It seeks to constitute a state that exists to serve the common good, where the democratic processes of *government of and by the people* are reliably translated into tangible developmental outcomes *for the people*. Such a state – a strong democracy serving the people like never before – is certainly an attractive, exciting, proposition.

Given the practical difficulties of establishing such an independent Northumbrian state, however, one might well wonder whether it is too far-fetched. It must be admitted, from the outset, that the draft constitution contained in this book is a work of constitutional fiction, perhaps even of constitutional fantasy. Drafting pretend constitutions for the illumination of a Constituent Assembly not chosen, under a Constitutional Transition Act not enacted, for a country that does not exist, is a bizarre form of political engagement at the best of times.

Yet this draft constitution might be seen more in the spirit of a catalyst to hasten constitutional change. In drafting it, I am not necessarily endorsing Northumbrian independence. I am endorsing the restoration and renewal of constitutional democracy, the refoundation of our institutions, and the expansion of the constitutional imagination. Much of this draft could be applicable, with relatively minor changes, to an independent Scotland or Wales. With bigger changes – perhaps the retention of a figurehead monarchy, and a more developed scheme of devolution – it might inform constitutional design options for the United Kingdom, or better still an independent England.

It is therefore hoped that this draft constitution, even if it does not advance Northumbria's independence, might at least admit the North's legitimate grievances, and support its claim to power, resources and recognition, while also advancing the 'Good Old Cause' of constitutional democracy and good governance across the whole of the British nations.

DRAFT CONSTITUTION FOR A REPUBLIC OF NORTHUMBRIA

PART I. THE REPUBLIC

1. Foundational Values and Commitments

(1)   Northumbria is a sovereign, social, democratic and parliamentary Republic, founded upon values that recognise the sovereignty of God, human dignity and equality, mutuality and solidarity, justice and compassion, concern for the common good, care for nature and the environment, and respect for each person's freedom, integrity and moral responsibility.

(2)   The Republic is committed to –
   (a)   representative and responsible parliamentary democracy;
   (b)   constitutionalism, respect for human rights and the rule of law;
   (c)   an independent, impartial, competent and accessible system of justice;
   (d)   good governance, including integrity, transparency and accountability;
   (e)   the encouragement of inclusive and sustainable economic development;
   (f)   democratic decentralisation in accordance with the concept of subsidiarity; and
   (g)   the maintenance of a free, pluralist, open society in which individuals and communities can flourish in their diversity.

(3)   All persons interpreting or applying this Constitution or
        any law or regulation, shall interpret or apply it, so far
        as it is reasonably practicable to do so, in ways that are
        congruent to the values and commitments declared in
        this section.

2. Supreme Law

(1)   This Constitution shall be the supreme law of
        Northumbria.

(2)   Any existing law and any law passed after the date of
        coming into force of this Constitution which is
        inconsistent with this Constitution shall, to the extent of
        the inconsistency, be void.

3. Territory

(1)   The territory of Northumbria shall include all those
        parts of England which immediately before the
        appointed day comprised the NUTS1 statistical regions
        of Yorkshire and the Humber, the North East and the
        North West, and the territorial waters belonging thereto
        in accordance with international law.

(2)   The City of York shall be the ceremonial capital of
        Northumbria and the seat of the President, but provision
        may be made by law for the Legislative Assembly, the
        Government, the Supreme Court, and other public
        institutions, to be located in other parts of Northumbria.

4. Citizenship and Residence

(1)   All persons who immediately before the appointed day were citizens of the United Kingdom of Great Britain and Northern Ireland shall on the appointed day become citizens of the Republic of Northumbria if –

        (a)   they are ordinarily resident in Northumbria on the appointed day;

        (b)   they were born in Northumbria, or either of their parents were born in Northumbria; or

        (c)   they are married or in a civil partnership with a person who is a Northumbria citizen under paragraphs (a) or (b).

(2)   Parliament may make further provision by law for the acquisition of Northumbrian citizenship by birth, marriage or naturalization; provided that such provision shall not unfairly discriminate on the grounds of race, ethnic origin, colour, religion, sex, age, or mental or physical disability.

(3)   No person who is Northumbrian citizen may ever be deprived of that citizenship except by means of an act of voluntary renunciation; Parliament may make provision by law for the voluntary renunciation of citizenship, but no person shall renounce such citizenship if the effect of that renunciation would render that person, or any spouse, child or other dependent of that person, stateless.

(4)   A person who is a Northumbrian citizen, or who is entitled to be registered as a Northumbria citizen, and is also a citizen of some other country, shall not solely on

the ground that he or she is or becomes a citizen of another country –

(a)   be deprived of his or her Northumbrian citizenship, refused registration as a Northumbria citizen, or required to renounce citizenship of that other country;

(b)   be refused a Northumbrian passport, or have such a passport withdrawn, cancelled, or impounded solely the ground that he or she is in possession of a passport issued by some other country of which he or she is a citizen; or

(c)   be required to surrender or be prohibited from acquiring a passport issued by some other country of which he or she is a citizen being issued with a Northumbrian passport or as a condition of retaining such a passport.

(5)   All persons ordinarily resident in Northumbria on the appointed day shall have the right to continue in residence in Northumbrian and to return to residence in Northumbria after any period or periods of absence, whether they exercise or renounce their rights to Northumbrian citizenship; and all children under the age of eighteen years on the appointed day who have at least one parent whose principal residence is in Northumbrian on the appointed day shall have the same rights as though they had been resident in Northumbria at that date.

5. National Symbols

(1)   The national flag of Northumbria is the Flag of St Oswald.

(2) The national anthem of Northumbria shall be 'True North'.

(3) The national motto of Northumbria shall be *'ubi stercus, ibi aes'*.

6. Official Language

(1) English shall be the official language, and subject to the following provisions of this section, shall be the working language of Parliament, the public administration and the courts.

(2) Provision shall be made according to law for the use of Braille and British Sign Language as auxiliary languages for the benefit of blind, partially sighted, deaf or hard of hearing persons.

PART II. FUNDAMENTAL RIGHTS AND LIBERTIES

7. Right to Life

(1) Everyone's right to life shall be protected by law.

(2) No one shall be sentenced to death or executed.

(3) A person shall not be regarded as having been deprived of his or her life in contravention of this section if he or she dies –
   (a) as a result of a lawful act of war; or
   (b) from the use, to such extent and in such circumstances as are permitted by law, of such force as is reasonably justifiable –

     (i)   for the defence of any person from violence or for the defence of property;

    (ii)   in order to effect a lawful arrest or to prevent the escape of a person lawfully detained; or

    (iii)   for the purpose of suppressing a riot, insurrection or mutiny.

8. Prohibition of Torture

No one shall be subjected to torture or to inhuman or degrading treatment or punishment.

9. Prohibition of Slavery and Forced Labour

(1)   No one shall be held in slavery or servitude.

(2)   No one shall be required to perform forced or compulsory labour.

(3)   For the purpose of this section the term "forced or compulsory labour" shall not include:

    (a)   any work, not of a hazardous, demeaning or exploitative nature, required to be done in the ordinary course of detention imposed according to the provisions of section 10 or during conditional release from such detention;

    (b)   any service of a military character imposed by Act of Parliament during time of war or threat of invasion, or, in case of conscientious objectors, civilian service exacted instead of compulsory military service;

(c)   any service exacted in case of an emergency or calamity threatening the life or well-being of the community;

(d)   any work or service which forms part of normal civic obligations.

10. Right to Personal Liberty and Security

(1)   Everyone has the right to liberty and security of person. No one shall be deprived of his or her liberty save in the following cases and in accordance with a procedure prescribed by law:

(a)   the lawful detention of a person after conviction by a competent court;

(b)   the lawful arrest or detention of a person for non-compliance with the lawful order of a court or in order to secure the fulfilment of any obligation prescribed by law;

(c)   the lawful arrest or detention of a person effected for the purpose of bringing him before the competent legal authority on reasonable suspicion of having committed an offence or when it is reasonably considered necessary to prevent his committing an offence or fleeing after having done so;

(d)   the detention of a minor by lawful order for the purpose of educational supervision or his lawful detention for the purpose of bringing him before the competent legal authority;

(e)   the lawful detention of persons for the prevention of the spreading of infectious diseases, of persons of unsound mind, alcoholics or drug addicts or vagrants;

(f)   the lawful arrest or detention of a person to prevent his effecting an unauthorised entry into the country or of a person against whom action is being taken with a view to deportation or extradition.

(2)   Everyone who is arrested shall be informed promptly, in a language which he or she understands, of the reasons for his arrest and of any charge against him.

(3)   Everyone arrested or detained in accordance with the provisions of paragraph (c) of subsection (1) of this section shall be brought promptly before a judge or other officer authorised by law to exercise judicial power and shall be entitled to trial within a reasonable time or to release pending trial. Release may be conditioned by reasonable guarantees to appear for trial.

(4)   Everyone who is deprived of his liberty by arrest or detention shall be entitled to take proceedings by which the lawfulness of his or her detention shall be decided speedily by a court and his or her release ordered if the detention is not lawful.

(5)   Everyone who has been the victim of arrest or detention in contravention of the provisions of this article shall have an enforceable right to compensation.

(6)   No one shall be deprived of his or her liberty merely on the ground of inability to full a contractual obligation.

11. Right to a Fair Trial

(1)   In the determination of his or her civil rights and obligations or of any criminal charge against him or her, everyone is entitled to a fair and public hearing within a reasonable time by an independent and impartial tribunal established by law. Judgment shall be pronounced publicly but the press and public may be excluded from all or part of the trial in the interest of morals, public order or national security in a democratic society, where the interests of juveniles or the protection of the private life of the parties so require, or the extent strictly necessary in the opinion of the court in special circumstances where publicity would prejudice the interests of justice.

(2)   Everyone charged with a criminal offence shall be presumed innocent until proved guilty according to law.

(3)   Everyone charged with a criminal offence has the following minimum rights:
   (a)   to be informed promptly, in a language which he understands and in detail, of the nature and cause of the accusation against him or her;
   (b)   to have adequate time and the facilities for the preparation of his or her defence;
   (c)   to defend himself in person or through legal assistance of his or her own choosing or, if he or she has not sufficient means to pay for legal assistance, to be given it free when the interests of justice so require;
   (d)   to examine or have examined witnesses against him or her and to obtain the attendance and examination of witnesses on his or her behalf

under the same conditions as witnesses against him or her;

(e) to have the free assistance of an interpreter if he or she cannot understand or speak the language used in court.

12. No Punishment without Law

(1) No one shall be held guilty of any criminal offence on account of any act or omission which did not constitute a criminal offence under national or international law at the time when it was committed. Nor shall a heavier penalty be imposed than the one that was applicable at the time the criminal offence was committed.

(2) This section shall not prejudice the trial and punishment of any person for any act or omission which, at the time when it was committed, was criminal according to the general principles of law recognised by civilised nations.

13. Right of Appeal in Criminal Matters

(1) Everyone convicted of a criminal offence by a tribunal shall have the right to have his conviction or sentence reviewed by a higher tribunal. The exercise of this right, including the grounds on which it may be exercised, shall be governed by law.

(2) This right may be subject to exceptions in regard to offences of a minor character, as prescribed by law, or in cases in which the person concerned was tried in the first instance by the highest tribunal or was convicted following an appeal against acquittal.

14. Compensation for Wrongful Conviction

When a person has by a final decision been convicted of a criminal offence and when subsequently his conviction has been reversed, or he or she has been pardoned, on the ground that a new or newly discovered fact shows conclusively that there has been a miscarriage of justice, the person who has suffered punishment as a result of such conviction shall be compensated according to law, unless it is proved that the nondisclosure of the unknown fact in time is wholly or partly attributable to him or her.

15. Right Not to be Tried or Punished Twice

(1) No one shall be liable to be tried or punished again in criminal proceedings for an offence for which he or she has already been finally acquitted or convicted in accordance with the law.

(2) The provisions of subsection (1) shall not prevent the reopening of the case in accordance with the law and penal procedure, if there is evidence of new or newly discovered facts, or if there has been a fundamental defect in the previous proceedings, which could affect the outcome of the case.

16. Right to Respect for Private and Family Life

(1)   Everyone has the right to respect for his or her private and family life, home and correspondence.

(2)   There shall be no interference by a public authority with the exercise of this right except such as is in accordance with the law and is necessary in a democratic society in the interests of national security, public safety or the economic well-being of the country, for the prevention of disorder or crime, for the protection of health or morals, or for the protection of the rights and freedoms of others.

17. Freedom of Thought, Conscience and Religion

(1)   Everyone has the right to freedom of thought, conscience and religion. This shall include freedom to change his or her religion or belief and freedom, either alone or in community with others and in public or private, to manifest his or her religion or belief, in worship, teaching, practice and observance.

(2)   Freedom to manifest one's religion or beliefs shall be subject only to such limitations as are prescribed by law and are necessary in a democratic society in the interests of public safety, for the protection of public order, health or morals, or for the protection of the rights and freedoms of others.

(3)   In the exercise of any functions which they assume in relation to education and to teaching, the public authorities shall respect the right of parents or legal guardians to ensure such education and teaching in

conformity with their own religious and philosophical convictions; this shall include the right of parents or guardians to home-school or privately educate their children.

18. Freedom of Expression

(1)   Everyone has the right to freedom of expression. This right shall include freedom to hold opinions and to receive and impart information and ideas without interference by public authority and regardless of frontiers.

(2)   The exercise of these freedoms, since it carries with it duties and responsibilities, may be subject to such formalities, conditions, restrictions or penalties as are prescribed by law and are necessary in a democratic society, in the interests of national security, territorial integrity or public safety, for the prevention of disorder or crime, for the protection of health or morals, for the protection of the reputation or rights of others, for preventing the disclosure of information received in confidence, or for maintaining the authority and impartiality of the judiciary.

(3)   Subsection (1) shall not prevent the public authorities from requiring the licensing of broadcasting, television or cinema enterprises according to law.

19. Freedom of Assembly and Association

(1)   Everyone has the right to freedom of peaceful assembly and to freedom of association with others, including the

right to form and to join trade unions for the protection
of his or her interests.

(2)   No restrictions shall be placed on the exercise of these
rights other than such as are prescribed by law and are
necessary in a democratic society in the interests of
national security or public safety, for the prevention of
disorder or crime, for the protection of health or morals
or for the protection of the rights and freedoms of
others.

20. Right to Vote

(1)   Subject to subsection (2), every person who is a citizen
of Northumbria who is at least eighteen years of age on
the date of the poll and resident in Northumbria shall be
entitled to be registered as a voter for, and to vote in,
referendums and in elections to Legislative Assembly
and to local authorities.

(2)   Parliament may by law restrict the right of a person to
be registered as a voter, to the extent justifiable in a free
and democratic society, only on the grounds that he or
she –
    (a)   is under legal guardianship on grounds of
insanity or severe mental incapacity;
    (b)   is serving a custodial sentence exceeding twelve
months' duration; or
    (c)   has an unspent conviction for an offence relating
to corruption or malpractice in elections or
referendums as prescribed by law.

21. Marriage Rights

(1)   Men and women of marriageable age have the right to marry and to found a family, according to the laws governing the exercise of this right.

(2)   Spouses shall enjoy equality of rights and responsibilities of a private law character between them, and in their relations with their children, as to marriage, during marriage and in the event of its dissolution.

(3)   This section shall not prevent such laws being enacted as are necessary in the interests of children.

22. Protection of Property

(1)   Every natural or legal person is entitled to the peaceful enjoyment of his possessions. No one shall be deprived of his possessions except in the public interest and subject to the conditions provided for by law and by the general principles of international law.

(2)   Subsection (1) shall not, however, impair the right of the Parliament, or a local authority within its competence –
    (a)   to enact such laws as it may deem necessary to control the use of property in accordance with the general interest;
    (b)   to secure the payment of taxes or other contributions or penalties, or
    (c)   to bring utilities, infrastructure, public services, or strategic industries into public ownership,

provided that compensation is paid in advance at prevailing market rates.

23. Freedom of Movement

(1)   Everyone lawfully within the territory of Northumbria shall, within that territory, have the right to liberty of movement and freedom to choose his residence. Everyone shall be free to leave the country.

(2)   No restrictions shall be placed on the exercise of these rights other than such as are in accordance with law and are necessary in a democratic society in the interests of national security or public safety, for the maintenance of public order, for the prevention of crime, for the protection of health or morals, or for the protection of the rights and freedoms of others.

(3)   The rights set forth in subsection (1) of this section may also be subject, in particular areas, to restrictions imposed in accordance with law and justified by the public interest in a democratic society.

24. Right of Abode

(1)   No citizen of Northumbria shall be expelled, by means either of an individual or of a collective measure, from the territory of Northumbria.

(2)   No citizen of Northumbria shall be deprived of the right to enter the territory of Northumbria.

25. Procedural Safeguards Relating to the Expulsion of Aliens

(1)   Collective expulsion of aliens is prohibited.

(2)   An alien lawfully resident in the territory of Northumbria shall not be expelled therefrom except in pursuance of a decision reached in accordance with law and shall be allowed:
(a)   to submit reasons against his expulsion,
(b)   to have his case reviewed, and
(c)   to be represented for these purposes before the competent authority or a person or persons designated by that authority.

(3)   An alien may be expelled before the exercise of his or her rights under paragraphs (a), (b) and (c) of subsection (2) of this section, when such expulsion is necessary in the interests of public order or is grounded on reasons of national security.

26. Freedom of Information

(1)   Everyone has the right to freedom of information, including –
(a)   access to official files, documents, reports, statistics, and other information, in whatever form, and
(b)   access to any information held on them by the public authorities or by any private person or corporation under contract to or on behalf of any public authority.

(2)   No restrictions shall be placed on the right declared and recognised by this section, other than such restrictions prescribed by law as are necessary in a democratic society, in the interests of national security, territorial integrity or public safety, for the prevention of disorder or crime, for the protection of health or morals and of the reputation or the rights of others, privacy, prevention of contempt of court, protection of parliamentary privilege, for preventing the disclosure of information communicated in confidence, or for maintaining the authority and impartiality of the judiciary.

27. Prohibition of Discrimination

(1)   Every individual is equal before and under the law and has the right to the equal protection and equal benefit of the law without discrimination and, in particular, without discrimination based on race, national or ethnic origin, colour, religion, sex or gender, sexual orientation, age, or mental or physical disability.

(2)   Subsection (1) does not preclude any law, program or activity that has as its object the amelioration of conditions of disadvantaged individuals or groups including those that are disadvantaged because of race, national or ethnic origin, colour, religion, sex or gender, sexual orientation, age or mental or physical disability.

28. Limitations and Restriction on Rights

(1)   Nothing in this Part may be interpreted as implying for any public authority, group or person any right to

engage in any activity or perform any act aimed at the destruction of any of the rights and freedoms set forth herein or at their limitation to a greater extent than is provided for in this Part.

(2)   The restrictions permitted under this Part to the said rights and freedoms shall not be applied for any purpose other than those for which they have been prescribed.

29. Right to an Effective Remedy

(1)   Anyone whose rights or freedoms, as guaranteed by this Constitution, have been infringed or denied may apply to a court of competent jurisdiction to obtain such effective remedy as the court considers appropriate and just in the circumstances, notwithstanding that the violation has been committed by persons acting in an official capacity.

(2)   Where, in proceedings under subsection (1), a court concludes that evidence was obtained in a manner that infringed or denied any rights or freedoms guaranteed by this constitution, the evidence shall be excluded if it is established that, having regard to all the circumstances, the admission of it in the proceedings would bring the administration of justice into disrepute.

30. Existing Rights

The guarantee in this Constitution of certain rights and freedoms shall not be construed as denying the existence of any other rights or freedoms that exist by virtue of any statute or charter, or by common law.

31. Derogation of Rights in Emergencies

(1) The President, on the advice of the Prime Minister, may by proclamation declare that a state of emergency exists for the purposes of this section.

(2) A state of emergency may be declared on the grounds -
   (a) that the Northumbria is at war, or a state of war is imminent, or any part of the territory of Northumbria or of its allies in the British Isles is under threat of invasion or attack, or
   (b) that a public emergency has arisen as a result of natural disaster, flood, fire, outbreak of pestilence, outbreak of infectious disease or other calamity, whether similar to the foregoing or not, on such a scale as to be likely to endanger the public safety or to deprive the community, or any substantial portion of the community, of supplies or services essential to life.

(3) Every declaration of emergency shall expire at the expiration of a period of fourteen days from the date of the declaration, unless it has in the meantime been approved by a resolution of the Legislative Assembly supported by the votes of at two-thirds of the total membership thereof.

(4) A declaration of emergency that has been approved by a resolution of the Legislative Assembly in pursuance of subsection (3) of this section shall, subject to subsection (5), remain in force for a period of six

months or such shorter period as may be specified in the resolution, and that period may be renewed, by means of a resolution of the Legislative Assembly supported by the votes of three-fourths of its total membership, for further periods of not more than six months.

(5) A declaration of emergency may at any time be revoked —

(a) by the President acting on the advice of the Prime Minister; or

(b) by a resolution of the Legislative supported by the votes of a majority of its members.

(6) Parliament may provide by law, during any period when a declaration of emergency is in effect and to the extent reasonably justifiable for the purpose of dealing with the emergency, for the limitation of the rights guaranteed by section 10 (personal liberty and security), section 16 (respect for private and family life), section 19 (freedom of association and assembly), and section 23 (freedom of movement).

(7) Orders and regulations made under any law enacted under subsection (6) shall be laid before the Legislative Assembly as soon as may be practicable after coming into effect, and may be suspended or revoked by means of a resolution passed by a majority of the members thereof.

(8) Laws enacted under subsection (6), and all orders and regulations made under any such law, shall unless sooner repealed or revoked cease to have effect upon the expiration or revocation of a declaration of emergency, and any person detained under any such

law, regulation or order shall thereupon be released,
unless there are other lawful grounds for their
continued detention.

32. Human Rights Commission

(1) There shall be a Human Rights Commission which
shall consist of –
  (a) a Chairperson appointed by the President on the
      advice of the Prime Minister given with the
      concurrence of the Leader of the Opposition;
  (b) two Commissioners appointed by the President
      on the advice of the Public Service Commission;
  (c) one Commissioner to be appointed by the
      President on the advice of the Prime Minister;
  (d) one Commissioner to be appointed by the
      President on the advice of the Leader of the
      Opposition; and
  (e) one Commissioner to be appointed by the
      President on the advice of the leader of the
      largest parties represent in the Legislative
      Assembly other than the parties of the Prime
      Minister and the Leader of the Opposition.

(2) In making appointments to the Human Rights
Commission consideration shall be given to –
  (a) the integrity, independence and personal qualities
      of the candidates;
  (b) the relevant qualifications and experience of the
      candidates; and
  (c) the need to reflect the diversity of society,
      especially but not exclusively in terms of gender,
      class, ethnicity, religion and political perspective.

(3)   A person shall not be qualified to be appointed as a member of the Human Rights Commission if—

    (a)   he or she is, or has at any time during the five years immediately preceding his appointment been, a member of the Legislative Assembly or any local authority;

    (b)   he or she is, or has at any time during the said five years been, nominated as a candidate for election as a member of the Legislative Assembly or any local authority;

    (c)   he or she is, or has at any time during the said five years been, the holder of an office in, or the employee of, any registered political party.

(4)   A member of the Human Rights Commission shall not enter upon the duties of his or her office until he or she has taken and subscribed the Oath of Allegiance and the Oath of Office in the form set out in the First Schedule to this Constitution.

(5)   A member of the Human Rights Commission shall cease to hold office—

    (a)   if he or she submits his resignation in writing to the President;

    (b)   if any circumstances arise that, if he were not a member of the Commission, would cause him or her to be disqualified to be appointed as such; or

    (c)   if he or she is removed from office in accordance with subsection (6).

    (d)   at the expiration of six years from the date of his or her appointment.

(6)   The members of the Human Rights Commission may not be removed from office during his or her term of office except by a resolution of the Legislative

Assembly passed by a two-thirds majority of its members on the grounds of incapacity, neglect of duty, or gross misconduct.

(7) In case of the death, resignation, or removal of any of a member of the Human Rights Commission, the vacancy shall be filled as soon as may be practicable in accordance with subsection (1).

(8) The Human Rights Commission may continue to perform its functions notwithstanding any vacancy in its membership or the absence of any member: provided that any decisions of the Commission shall require the concurrence of a majority of all its members.

(9) The Human Rights Commission may regulate its own procedure and shall not be subject to the direction or control of any other person or authority.

33. Powers and Functions of Human Rights Commission

(1) Subject to this Constitution and in accordance with any provisions prescribed by Act of Parliament, the Human Rights Commission shall have responsibility for –

   (a) promoting the protection and observance of, and respect for, human rights;
   (b) providing or supporting civic education about the rights and freedoms recognised in this Constitution, as well as other internationally recognised rights and freedoms;

(c)   monitoring and reporting on the observance of human rights and on progress towards realisation of the Directive principles;

(d)   making recommendations to Ministers concerning any matter affecting the rights and freedoms recognised in this Constitution;

(e)   receiving and investigating complaints about alleged abuses of human rights and taking steps to secure appropriate redress if human rights have been violated, including making applications to the courts for redress or for other forms of relief or remedies;

(f)   making recommendations to the Government, the Legislative Assembly, or to local authorities, to improve the protection of human rights; and

(g)   performing any other functions or exercising any powers as are conferred on the Commission by law.

(2)   In the exercise of its functions under this Constitution or any law the Human Rights Commission shall not be subject to the direction or control of any other person or authority.

(3)   The Commission may regulate its own procedure and, with the consent of the Prime Minister, may confer powers or impose duties on any public officer or any authority of the Government of Northumbria for the purpose of the exercise of its functions.

PART III. DIRECTIVE PRINCIPLES

34. Protection of the Family

(1)   The Republic shall protect the family as the natural primary and fundamental group of society.

(2)   The public authorities may adopt policies to support marriage and to promote the material and moral wellbeing of families, including measures to achieve the eradication of child poverty.

35. Conservation and Countryside

(1)   The Republic shall endeavour to conserve and restore natural habitats; to prevent pollution and to maintain the purity of the air, soil and water; to sustainably manage natural resources; to promote bio-diversity and encourage wildlife; to prevent and mitigate the effects of climate change; and to safeguard and protect the environment of Northumbria for future generations.

(2)   The Republic shall promote public access to the countryside by the establishment of national parks; and Parliament shall provide by law for a 'right to roam' on open moors and public land.

36. Culture

The Republic shall protect the cultural traditions and heritage of the people, preserve historic sites and monuments, and promote the development and enrichment of Northumbrian culture.

37. Housing

The Republic shall be responsible for improving housing conditions and for ensuring that everyone has a right to decent housing and that no person is involuntarily made homeless.

38. Healthcare

The Republic shall be responsible for the promotion of public health and for the provision of a Northumbrian Health Service, freely accessible to all, to secure wellbeing and human dignity.

39. Education

The Republic, while respecting the rights of families to choose religious, private or home schooling, shall provide by law for free publicly-funded preschool, primary and secondary education, and shall provide financial support to encourage further and higher education.

40. Employment Rights

The Republic shall protect the rights of workers, including the right to form and join trade unions for the promotion of their interests, the right to collectively bargain, and the right to conditions of work which are fair and which respect the dignity of the person; in particular, it shall be the duty of Parliament to ensure by law that everyone has the right to safe and healthy conditions of work, to a decent living wage, and to adequate opportunities for rest and leisure.

41. Social Security and Pensions

(1)   The Republic shall ensure that every person who is unable to work by reason of age or physical or mental disability or infirmity, or because of family caring responsibilities, or because suitable employment is unavailable, has a right to be provided with reasonable alternative means of subsistence to be determined in accordance with law.

(2)   The Republic shall ensure that persons who have reached the retirement age prescribed by law shall have the right to public pensions sufficient to maintain their dignity and independence.

42. Industrial, Economic and Infrastructure Development

(1)   The Republic shall promote the inclusive, sustainable and equitable industrial and economic development of Northumbria, including rural development and urban regeneration, to increase national prosperity, to improve the quality of life of the people, and to eradicate poverty.

(2)   For the purposes of this section, Parliament may enact legislation to nationalise utilities, services and infrastructure, as well as industries of national economic or strategic importance, and to provide for

their operation by publicly-owned corporations for the national interest.

43. Applicability of Directive Principles

The provisions of this Part shall not be directly enforceable in any court, but the principles therein contained are nevertheless fundamental to the governance of the Republic; it shall be the duty of the Government, the Legislative Assembly, and local authorities, to apply these principles in the making and implementing laws; and the courts shall have regard to these principles in the interpretation and application of this Constitution and Acts of Parliament.

PART IV. THE PRESIDENT

44. Election of President

(1)   There shall be a President of Northumbria who shall be the Head of State.

(2)   The President shall be elected by the Legislative Assembly, by secret ballot, upon the proposal of the Nominating Committee established by this section.

(3)   The Nominating Committee shall consist of fifteen members, which shall include –
    (a)   the Speaker of the Legislative Assembly, as chair of the committee;
    (a)   the Prime Minister;
    (b)   the Leader of the Opposition; and

(c)   twelve shall be members of the Legislative Assembly, selected by random lot, in such manner as the Legislative Assembly may prescribe.

(3)   If the qualified candidate proposed by the Nominating Committee is approved by a two-thirds majority of the votes cast in the Legislative Assembly, he or she shall be elected President; but if, after two ballots, he or she is not, approved by two-thirds of the votes cast, the Nominating Committee shall propose a second candidate, who shall likewise be put to a vote of the Legislative Assembly, and shall be elected if approved by two-thirds of the votes cast.

(4)   If the second candidate is not, after two ballots, approved by two-thirds of the votes cast, the Nominating Committee shall be dissolved; a new Nominating Committee shall be selected, and a third qualified candidate shall be proposed to the Legislative Assembly. If that third candidate is approved by two-thirds of the votes cast, he or she shall be elected.

(5)   If after two ballots the third candidate has not been approved by two-thirds of the votes cast, the two candidates who, in the total aggregate of votes cast so far, have the highest total number of votes, shall go to the Legislative Assembly in a run-off election, also to be conducted by secret ballot, and the one who receives the most votes in the run-off election shall be elected.

(6)   The Nominating Committee may act notwithstanding any vacancy in its membership, and its proceedings shall not be invalidated by the absence of any member.

45. Qualifications and Disqualifications

(1)   A person shall be qualified to be elected as President if, and shall not be so qualified unless, he or she is qualified, and not disqualified, to be elected as a member of the Legislative Assembly.

(2)   A person shall not be qualified to be elected as President if he or she –
    (a)   has been removed from the office of President on grounds of misbehaviour, or
    (b)   has, within a period of seven years immediately preceding that appointment, held the office of Prime Minister or any ministerial office, or served as Leader of the Opposition.

46. Term of Office of President

(1)   Subject to this Constitution, the President shall hold office for a term of five years from the date on which he or she assumes office.

(2)   Notwithstanding the expiry of his or her term, the President shall continue to hold office until his or her successor assumes office, or for a period of ninety days, whichever is the shorter period.

(3)   A serving or former President, if otherwise qualified, may be reappointed for a second term; provided that no person may serve as President for more than two terms, nor be appointed to the office of President more than twice.

47. Restrictions on the President

The President shall not –
    (a)   hold any other office of profit or any other position carrying the right to remuneration for the rendering of services, nor engage in any occupation for reward, nor business venture, outside the functions of his or her office;
    (b)   be a member of any political party; nor
    (c)   leave the territory of Northumbria without first having the approval of the Prime Minister.

48. Resignation and Removal of the President

(1)   The President may resign his or her office, on grounds of illness or incapacity, or for other stated cause, by writing under his or her hand addressed to the Speaker of the Legislative Assembly, who shall forthwith advise the Prime Minister of that resignation.

(2)   The President may be removed from office by a resolution of the Legislative Assembly on the grounds of misbehaviour, or of incapacity; but no proposal for the removal of the President shall be effective unless –
    (a)   notice of motion setting out the grounds for the proposed removal has been given in writing and signed by not less than one-fourth of the total number of members of the Legislative Assembly (including vacancies);
    (b)   a period of at least fourteen days has elapsed between that notice and the debate on the motion; and

(c)   the motion has been agreed to by not less than two-thirds of the total number of Members of Parliament (including vacancies).

(3)   A resolution carried under the provisions of subsection (2), shall have the effect of removing the President from his or her office as from the date on which the resolution is so carried.

49. Vacancy, Absence or Incapacity

(1)   If a vacancy exists in the office of President, or during any period in which the President is absent from Northumbria or unable to perform his or her functions, the Chief Justice shall perform the functions of the President.

(2)   Whenever the Speaker of the Legislative Assembly declares in writing that he or she is satisfied by evidence (which shall include, where possible, the evidence of at least two physicians), that the President is by reason of infirmity of body or mind incapable for the time being of performing his or her functions, then, until it is declared in like manner that the President has so far recovered his or her health as to warrant his or her resumption of the functions of the office of President, those functions shall be performed by the Chief Justice.

(3)   If the President is incapable of performing his or her functions under subsection (2) for a period of ninety days continuously, he or she shall be deemed to have resigned on the ninetieth day.

50. Powers and Functions of the President

The only powers and functions of the President are those prescribed by this Constitution or by any law in effect in Northumbria under this Constitution, and such powers and functions shall be exercised solely in accordance with this Constitution and the law; provided, however, that as Head of State the President may perform ceremonial, civic, social and charitable duties, of a non-partisan nature, in accordance with the established traditions, customs and conventions of parliamentary government.

51. President to Act on Ministerial Advice

(1)   The President in the performance of his or her functions shall act on the binding advice of Cabinet, the Prime Minister or a responsible Minister, as the case may be.

(2)   Subsection (1) shall not apply to –
    (a)   those functions (known as 'reserve powers') which the President is authorised by this Constitution to exercise on his or her own deliberate judgment or personal discretion; or
    (b)   those functions which the President is required by this Constitution to exercise on the advice of, or after consultation with, the Speaker of the Legislative Assembly, the Public Service Commission, the Judicial Service Commission, or any other person or authority.

(3)   Where the President is authorised by this Constitution to exercise reserve powers after consultation with any person or authority, the President shall be bound to so

consult in good faith, but shall not be bound to act on the advice given.

(4)   Where the President is required by this Constitution to make an appointment on the advice of the Prime Minister given with the concurrence of the Leader of the Opposition, the following steps shall be taken –

    (a)   the Prime Minister shall first consult the Leader of the Opposition and thereafter tender his or her recommendation to the President;

    (b)   the President shall then inform the Leader of the Opposition of this recommendation and if the Leader of the Opposition concurs therein the President shall act on such recommendation;

    (c)   if the Leader of the Opposition does not concur in the recommendation, the President shall summon a meeting with the Prime Minister and the Leader of the Opposition, in which the Prime Minister and Leader of the Opposition shall seek to reach agreement;

    (d)   if as a result of that meeting or otherwise the Prime Minister and Leader of the Opposition tender a joint recommendation to the President, the President shall act on such recommendation;

    (e)   if no joint recommendation under paragraph (e) has been received within thirty days of the initial advice being tendered, then the President, after consulting the Prime Minister, the Leader of the Opposition, and the chair of the Public Service Commission, may make the appointment in his or her own deliberate judgment.

(5)   The question of whether the President has received or acted in accordance with advice under this section shall not be enquired into in any court of law; but the validity

and lawfulness of any act arising from such advice may nevertheless be subject to judicial review according to law.

(6)   If the President is required by subsection (1) or by law to exercise any power or to perform any function in accordance with the binding advice of any person or authority, and he or she does not so act within a period of seven days after the advice has been received by the President, or within such other period as the person or authority tendering that advice shall specify, then the President shall at the end of that period be deemed to have acted in accordance with the advice.

52. President to be Informed

It shall be the duty of the Prime Minister –
(a)   to arrange for the circulation to the President of copies of the agenda and minutes of Cabinet and of all other papers laid before Cabinet at the time when they are circulated to Ministers; and
(b)   to furnish such information relating to the administration of the affairs of Northumbria and proposals for legislation as the President may request.

53. Presidential Oaths

The President, before assuming the powers of his or her office, shall take and subscribe before the Chief Justice, or another member of the Supreme Court duly deputed for that purpose, the Oath of Allegiance and Oath of Office in the forms prescribed by the First Schedule.

59. Public Seal

The President shall keep and use the Public Seal of Northumbria.

60. Salary and Allowances of President

The salary and allowances of the President shall be determined by Act of Parliament and shall be charged on the Consolidated Fund; and any alteration of the salary or allowances of the President shall not apply to the President in office at the time such alteration is approved.

61. President's Staff

(1)   Parliament may from time to time prescribe the offices that are to constitute the personal staff of the President, the salaries and allowances that are to be paid to the members of that staff and the other sums that are to be paid in respect of the expenditure attaching to the office of the President; and any salaries or other sums prescribed under this subsection shall be charged on the Consolidated Fund.

(2)   The power to make appointments to the offices for the time being prescribed under subsection (1) as offices on the official staff of the President, and to remove and to exercise disciplinary control over persons holding or acting in any such offices, shall vest in the President acting in his or her discretion after consultation with the Chairperson of the Public Service Commission.

PART V. THE EXECUTIVE

62. Executive Power

(1)   The executive authority of Northumbria shall be vested in the President and subject to the provisions of this Constitution shall be exercised by the President or by the Cabinet or any Minister authorised by the Cabinet, either directly or through officers subordinate to them.

(2)   Nothing in this section shall prevent Parliament from conferring executive functions on other persons or authorities by law.

63. Cabinet

(1)   There shall be a Cabinet of Northumbria which shall consist of the Prime Minister, the Deputy Prime Minister, and such other Ministers as the President acting upon the advice of the Prime Minister may from time to time summon and appoint to the Cabinet.

(2)   The Cabinet shall be the principal instrument of policy and shall be charged with the general direction and control of the Government and shall be collectively responsible to the Legislative Assembly.

(3)   The Prime Minister (or in the absence thereof the Deputy Prime Minister or such other Minister as the Prime Minister may deputise for the time being for that purpose) shall summon and set the agenda for the Cabinet, preside over its sessions, and ensure the execution of its decisions.

64. Appointment of Ministers

(1)   Whenever there is an occasion to appoint a Prime Minister, the President shall appoint to that office the person who has been duly nominated as Prime Minister by a resolution of the Legislative Assembly.

(3)   The President, acting on the advice of the Prime Minister, shall appoint the other Ministers.

(4)   The total number of persons holding ministerial office (including the Prime Minister, Deputy Prime Minister, Ministers in Cabinet, and Ministers not in the Cabinet, however designated) shall not exceed one-fifth of the total membership of the Legislative Assembly.

(5)   Except as provided in subsection (6), the Prime Minister and the other Ministers shall be appointed only from amongst the members of the Legislative Assembly, and any other appointment shall be void.

(6)   If Parliament is dissolved a person who was a member of the Legislative Assembly immediately before the dissolution may be appointed to, or continue to hold, office as Prime Minister or as another Minister, for a period of up to sixty days after the day on which the Legislative Assembly meets following the general election after such dissolution, after which he or she shall cease to hold such office unless he or she is a member of the Legislative Assembly.

65. Removal of Ministers

(1)   If the Legislative Assembly passes a resolution supported by the votes of a majority of all the members of the Assembly declaring that it has no confidence in the Government and the Prime Minister does not within five days after the passing of that resolution resign, the President shall remove the Prime Minister from office; provided, that the President shall not remove the Prime Minister under this subsection if within the said period of five days the Legislative Assembly is dissolved.

(2)   The defeat of the Government on a vote in reply to the President's Speech under section 96, shall be treated as a vote of no confidence. Subsection (1) shall be applied accordingly.

(3)   If, at any time between a general election to the Legislative Assembly and the first meeting of the Legislative Assembly thereafter, the President in his or her deliberate judgment considers that, in consequence of changes in the membership of the Legislative Assembly resulting from that election, the Prime Minister will no longer be able to command the support of the majority of the members of the Assembly, the President may remove the Prime Minister from office.

(4)   The Prime Minister shall also cease to hold office –
    (a)   upon his or her death,
    (b)   if he or she tenders his or her resignation in writing to the President, or
    (c)   if he or she ceases to be a member of the Legislative Assembly otherwise than by reason of the dissolution of the Legislative Assembly.

(5)   A Minister other than the Prime Minister shall cease to hold office –

   (a)   upon his or her death,

   (b)   if he or she tenders his or her resignation in writing to the President and if the President, acting on the advice of the Prime Minister, accepts his or her resignation;

   (c)   if the President, acting on the advice of the Prime Minister, dismisses him or her,

   (d)   if he or she ceases to be a member of Parliament otherwise than by reason of the dissolution of Parliament, or

   (e)   upon the appointment of a new Prime Minister.

(6)   A Prime Minister who resigns, is dismissed, or otherwise ceases to hold office shall, if directed by the President on his or her own deliberate judgment, continue to perform his or her duties, in a caretaker capacity, until he or she is re-appointed, or until his or her successor is appointed.

66. Absence, Incapacity or Vacancy of the Prime Minister

(1)   If the Prime Minister is absent from Northumbria or is by reason of illness or for other cause unable to perform the functions of his or her office, the President may authorize the Deputy Prime Minister, or if the Deputy Prime Minister is unavailable some other member of the Cabinet, to perform the functions of Prime Minister, until that authorisation is revoked.

(2)   The President's functions under subsection (1) shall be performed on the advice of the Prime Minister, if there is a Prime Minister in office and if the Prime Minister is

capable of tendering such advice; otherwise, they shall be performed by the President on the advice of the Cabinet.

(3)   If the Prime Minister dies in office, the President on the advice of the Cabinet shall authorise the Deputy Prime Minister, or if the Deputy Prime Minister is unavailable another member of the Cabinet, to perform the functions of Prime Minister until a Prime Minister is appointed.

67. Allocation of Portfolios

The President, on the advice of the Prime Minister, may, by directions in writing, charge the Prime Minister or any other Minister with responsibility for any business of the Government, including the administration of any department thereof; and each Minister shall be individually responsible for his or her personal conduct and for the administration of the department under his or her charge.

68. Leave of Absence and Acting Ministers

(1)   The President, acting in accordance with the advice of the Prime Minister, may grant leave of absence from his or her duties to any Minister other than the Prime Minister.

(2)   Whenever any Minister is for any cause unable to perform any of the functions of his office, whether or not leave of absence has been requested or granted, the President on the advice of the Prime Minister may

appoint any other person qualified to hold ministerial office to act in the said Minister's stead, either generally or in the performance of any particular function.

69. Oaths to be taken by Ministers

A person on being appointed to ministerial office shall before entering upon the duties of his or her office take and subscribe the Oath of Allegiance and Oath of Office in the forms prescribed by the First Schedule.

70. Secretary to the Cabinet

(1)   There shall be a Secretary to the Cabinet, who shall be a public officer.

(2)   The Secretary to the Cabinet shall have charge of the Cabinet Office and shall be responsible, in accordance with such instructions as may be given to him or her by the Prime Minister, for arranging the business for, and keeping the minutes of, the Cabinet, and for conveying the decisions of the Cabinet to the appropriate person or authority, and shall have such other functions as the Prime Minister may direct.

71. Permanent Secretaries

Where a Minister has been charged with responsibility for any department of the Government, he or she shall exercise general direction and control over that department; and, subject to such direction and control, the department shall be under the supervision of a senior public officer (in this Constitution referred to as a Permanent Secretary) appointed for that purpose.

72. Ministerial Code

(1)   There shall be a Ministerial Code, which shall provide authoritative official guidance on –
    (a)   the procedures and practices of the Cabinet;
    (b)   the duties and responsibilities of Ministers;
    (c)   the relationship between Ministers and Civil Servants,
    (d)   the relationship between Ministers and the Legislative Assembly, and
    (e)   the standards of ethics, conduct, behaviour and integrity expected of Minsters.

(2)   The Secretary to the Cabinet, under the direction of the Prime Minister, may propose revisions to the Ministerial Code and shall cause each draft revision to be published and laid before the Legislative Assembly; and such revisions to the Ministerial Code shall come into effect only after having been approved by a resolution of the Legislative Assembly.

73. Attorney-General

(1)   There shall be an Attorney-General whose office shall be a ministerial office of Cabinet rank and who, subject to this section, shall be appointed by the President on the advice of the Prime Minister in accordance with section 64.

(2)   No person shall be appointed as Attorney-General
       unless he or she is qualified to be appointed as a judge
       of the senior courts of Northumbria.

(3)   Subsection (5) of section 64 shall not apply to the
       appointment of the Attorney-General.

(4)   The Attorney-General may sit and speak in the
       Legislative Assembly even if he or she is not a member
       thereof, but may vote only if he or she is a member of
       the Legislative Assembly.

(5)   It shall be the duty of the Attorney-General to give
       advice to the Government upon such legal matters, and
       to perform such other duties of a legal character as may
       be referred or assigned to him or her by the Cabinet or
       by the Prime Minister; and in the performance of his or
       her duties the Attorney-General shall have the right of
       audience in all courts and tribunals in Northumbria.

(6)   The Attorney-General, while continuing in that office,
       shall not engage in any private practice.

74. Director of Public Prosecutions

(1)   There shall be a Director of Public Prosecutions who
       shall be a public officer and who shall be appointed by
       the President on the advice of the Prime Minister given
       after consultation with the Public Service Commission.

(2)   No person shall be appointed as Director of Public
       Prosecutions unless he or she possesses such legal
       qualifications and experience as may be prescribed by
       an Act of Parliament.

(3)   Unless he or she resigns in writing to the President, or is removed under subsection (4), the Director of Public Prosecutions shall serve for a term of four years and may be reappointed.

(4)   The Director of Public Prosecutions may be removed from office by the President, acting on the advice of the Prime Minister, after consultation with the Public Service Commission, on grounds of incapacity, neglect of duty, misconduct, or disqualification; and if the Director of Public Prosecutions is removed from office the Prime Minister shall cause the circumstances of the removal to be communicated without delay to the Legislative Assembly.

(5)   Director of Public Prosecutions shall have the power in any case in which he or she considers it desirable so to do –
    (a)   to institute criminal proceedings against any person before any court of law (other than a court-martial) in respect of any offence alleged to have been committed by that person;
    (b)   to take over and continue any such criminal proceedings that have been instituted or undertaken by any other person or authority; and
    (c)   to discontinue at any stage before judgment is delivered any such criminal proceedings instituted or undertaken by himself or any other person or authority.

(6)   The powers conferred on the Director of Public Prosecutions by paragraphs (b) and (c) of subsection (5) shall be vested in him or her to the exclusion of any other person or authority: provided that where any other

person or authority has instituted criminal proceedings, nothing in this subsection shall prevent the withdrawal of those proceedings by or at the instance of that person or authority and with the leave of the court.

(7)   For the purposes of this section, any appeal from a judgment in criminal proceedings before any court, or any case stated or question of law reserved for the purpose of any such proceedings to any other court, shall be deemed to be part of those proceedings: provided that the power conferred on the Director of Public Prosecutions by paragraph (c) of subsection (5) shall not be exercised in relation to any appeal by a person convicted in any criminal proceedings or to any case stated or question of law reserved at the instance of such a person.

75. Prerogative of Mercy

(1)   The President may –
   (a)   grant to any person convicted of any offence a pardon, either free or subject to lawful conditions;
   (b)   grant to any person a respite, either indefinite or for a specified period, from the execution of any punishment imposed on that person for such an offence;
   (c)   substitute a less severe form of punishment for that imposed on any person for such an offence; or
   (d)   remit the whole or part of any punishment imposed on any person for such an offence or any penalty or forfeiture otherwise due to the State on account of such an offence.

(2)   The powers of the President under subsection (1) shall
        be exercised on the advice of the Advisory Committee
        on the Prerogative of Mercy, which shall consist of –
        (a)   the Minister responsible for Justice, as
                chairperson;
        (b)   the Attorney-General;
        (c)   three other suitably qualified and experienced
                persons appointed by the President on the advice
                of the Prime Minister with the concurrence of the
                Leader of the Opposition, at least one of whom
                shall be a probation officer or social worker and
                at least one of whom shall be a medical
                practitioner.

(3)   Further provision on the composition, tenure,
        organisation and functioning of the Advisory
        Committee on the Prerogative of Mercy may be made
        by Act of Parliament.

PART VI. PARLIAMENT

Division I. Establishment of Parliament

76. Parliament

There shall be a Parliament of Northumbria, which
shall consist of the President and the Legislative
Assembly.

77. Legislative Authority

(1)   Subject to this Constitution, Parliament may enact, amend and repeal laws for the peace, order and good government of the whole or any part of Northumbria, including laws of extra-territorial effect.

(2)   Acts of Parliament may provide for the delegation to any person or authority of power to make orders-in-council, regulations and other secondary legislation, and for the control of the use of any such power by means of a requirement of legislative approval, or by means of a power to disallow, or in some other prescribed way; provided, that such delegation shall be for stated purposes specified in the Act of Parliament, and no general 'Enabling Act' shall be enacted.

Division II. Legislative Assembly

78. Composition of Legislative Assembly

(1)   The Legislative Assembly shall consist of two hundred members, who shall be elected by the persons registered to vote in accordance with section 20, according to the Single Transferable Vote system of proportional representation.

(2)   For the purpose of elections to the Legislative Assembly the territory of Northumbria shall be divided, in accordance with section 145, into forty electoral constituencies, each returning five members.

79. Qualifications for Membership

(1) Subject to subsection (2), a person shall be qualified for election as a member of the Legislative Assembly, and shall not be so qualified unless, at the date of his or her election —
(a) he or she has attained the age of eighteen years;
(b) he or she is a citizen of Northumbria, and
(c) he or she is registered in some constituency as a voter in elections of the Legislative Assembly and is not disqualified from voting in such elections.

(2) No person shall be qualified to be a member of, or to be nominated for election to, the Legislative Assembly if he or she —
(a) is, by virtue of his or her own act, under any acknowledgment of allegiance, obedience or adherence to any foreign power or state;
(b) is, under any law, adjudged to be of unsound mind;
(c) is an undischarged bankrupt, having been adjudged or otherwise declared bankrupt under any law;
(d) is under a sentence of imprisonment (by whatever name called) for a term of or exceeding twelve months;
(e) has at any time in the previous five years been convicted by any court of any offence that is connected with corrupt or illicit electoral practices and is prescribed by law as a disqualifying offence;
(f) is a member of the Electoral and Boundaries Commission, or the holder of any other office specified by law the functions of which involve

responsibility for, or in connection with, the conduct of any election to the Legislative Assembly or any local authority;

(g)   is the President, a public officer, a judge, a serving member of any of the Armed Forces, a police officer, or the holder of any other office in the service of the Republic which disqualifies him or her from membership of the Legislative Assembly under any Act of Parliament; or

(h)   has an interest in any contract with the Government of Northumbria that is proscribed by or in accordance with an Act of Parliament.

(3)   For the purposes of subsection (2)(d) of this section –

(a)   two or more terms of imprisonment that are required to be served consecutively shall be regarded as a single term of imprisonment for the aggregate period of those terms; and

(b)   no account shall be taken of a sentence of imprisonment imposed as an alternative to or in default of the payment of a fine.

(4)   No person may at any election be a candidate for more than one constituency.

80. Tenure of Office

(1)   Every member of the Legislative Assembly shall cease to be a member at the next dissolution of the Legislative Assembly after he or she has been elected.

(2)   The seat of a member of the Legislative Assembly shall also become vacant –

(a)   upon his or her death;

(b)   if he or she resigns his or her seat by writing
        under his or her hand addressed to the Speaker;

(c)   if he or she fails to attend sittings of the
        Legislative Assembly for two consecutive
        months of any session, except in so far as
        permission for reasonable absence may be
        granted in accordance with the Standing Orders
        of the Legislative Assembly;

(c)   if he or she ceases to be qualified, or becomes,
        disqualified for membership of the Legislative
        Assembly under the provisions of section 79;

(d)   in the circumstances prescribed by section 81
        (removal on changing party); or

(e)   in the circumstances prescribed by section 82
        (removal by recall).

81. Removal of Member on Changing Party

(1)   A member of the Legislative Assembly who is elected
        as a member of a political party and who voluntarily
        resigns from that party to sit as an independent or to
        join another party, shall cease to be a member of the
        Legislative Assembly twelve months after the date on
        which he or she gives notice to the Speaker that he or
        she has ceased to be a member of the original party.

(2)   Subsection (1) shall not have effect if, within that
        period of twelve months –
        (a)   the Legislative Assembly is dissolved and the
                member is re-elected in a general election;
        (b)   the member resigns from the Legislative
                Assembly and is re-elected in a by-election; or
        (c)   the member rejoins his or her original party.

(3) Subsection (1) shall not apply to a member -

    (a) solely on the grounds that he or she defies or votes against the party whip, or abstains from voting, or speaks against the party's leadership, without resigning from the party;

    (b) who is expelled from his or her original party against his or her will.

(4) In this section, 'original party' means the party to which a member belonged at the time of his or her most recent election as a member of the Legislative Assembly.

82. Removal of Member by Recall

(1) A member of the Legislative Assembly may be recalled by means of a recall petition on the grounds that the member -

    (a) has, after becoming a member of the Legislative Assembly, been found guilty of a criminal offence and sentenced or ordered to be imprisoned or detained;

    (b) has been ordered to be suspended from the sittings of the Legislative Assembly for a period of at least ten sitting days following a report from the Committee on Standards and Privileges; or

    (c) has, after becoming a member of the Legislative Assembly, been convicted of an offence of providing false or misleading information for allowances claims under any law in effect in Northumbria.

(2) As soon as reasonably practicable after becoming aware that any of the grounds of recall has been met in

relation to a member of the Legislative Assembly, the Speaker must give notice of that fact to the Electoral and Boundaries Commission, which shall arrange for a recall petition to be opened in the member's constituency; provided, that the foregoing shall not apply to any member who becomes subject to recall within a period of six months ending with the date on which Parliament is to be dissolved under subsection (1) of section 103, nor to any member who is already subject to a recall petition process, nor if the seat has already been vacated.

(4)　A recall petition shall be available for signature during a signing period of ninety days.

(5)　A recall petition be successful if signed within the signing period by not less than one-tenth of the registered electors in the constituency.

(6)　If a recall petition is successful, the seat of the member to which it applies shall, unless it has already been vacated, be vacant.

(7)　Parliament may make further provision by law for the implementation of this section.

83. Speaker and Deputy Speaker

(1)　There shall be a Speaker and a Deputy Speaker of the Legislative Assembly.

(2)　The Legislative Assembly shall, immediately when it first meets after a general election and as soon as possible after any vacancy occurs in the office of

Speaker or Deputy Speaker otherwise than by reason of a dissolution of Parliament, elect by secret ballot a Member of the Legislative Assembly to be Speaker, or Deputy Speaker as the case may be, of the Legislative Assembly.

(3)   The Speaker and the Deputy Speaker may at any time resign his or her office by writing under his or her hand addressed to the Clerk of the Legislative Assembly and shall vacate his or her office if he or she ceases to be a Member of the Legislative Assembly or if he or she is appointed to be a Minister.

(4)   The Speaker or the Deputy Speaker may be removed from office, on grounds of incapacity, gross misconduct, or for other stated cause, by a resolution passed by a two-thirds majority of the members of the Legislative Assembly.

(5)   Subject to the provisions of this Constitution, the functions conferred under the provisions of this Constitution upon the Speaker shall, if there is no person holding the office of Speaker or if the Speaker is absent from Northumbria or is otherwise unable to perform those functions, be performed by the Deputy Speaker.

84. Clerk and Officers of the Legislative Assembly

(1)   There shall be a Clerk of the Legislative Assembly and such other officers of the Assembly as may be required by law, whose powers and functions shall be prescribed, subject to any Act of Parliament, by the

Legislative Assembly.

(2)   Parliament may, by law, regulate the recruitment and
       conditions of service of the Clerk and other officers of
       the Legislative Assembly.

85. Determination of Questions as to Membership

(1)   The High Court shall have jurisdiction to hear and
       determine any question whether -
       (a)   any person has been validly elected as a member
              of the Legislative Assembly; or
       (b)   any member of the Legislative Assembly has
              vacated his or her seat.

(2)   Any application to the High Court for the determination
       of any question under subsection (1) may be made by -
       (a)   any person entitled to vote in the election to
              which the application relates;
       (b)   any person who was a candidate at the election to
              which the application relates;
       (c)   any member of the Legislative Assembly; or
       (d)   the Attorney-General.

(3)   If any application is made by a person other than the
       Attorney-General to the High Court for the
       determination of any question under this section, the
       Attorney-General may intervene and may then appear
       or be represented in the proceedings.

(4)   An appeal shall lie as of right to the Court of Appeal
       from any final decision of the High Court determining
       such a question as is referred to in subsection (1).

(5)   Parliament may make further provision by law for –
        (a)   the manner and circumstances, manner, and
                conditions upon which any application may be
                made to the High Court for the determination of
                any question under this section; and
        (b)   the powers, practice and procedure of the High
                Court and the Court of Appeal in relation to any
                such application.

(6)   In the exercise of his or her functions under this section
        the Attorney-General shall not be subject to the
        direction or control of any other person or authority.

86. Vacancies in the Legislative Assembly

Whenever the seat of a member of the Legislative
Assembly becomes vacant, other than by means of a
dissolution, the Speaker shall, unless Parliament is
sooner dissolved, order the Clerk to issue writs for a by-
election to be held no sooner than sixty days, but within
ninety days, of the vacancy arising.

Division III. Privileges and Procedures

87. Oath of members of the Legislative Assembly

Except for the purpose of enabling this section to be
complied with and for the election of a Speaker and
Deputy Speaker, no member of the Legislative
Assembly shall sit or vote therein until he or she shall
have taken and subscribed the Oath of Allegiance and
the Oath of Office as set out in the First Schedule.

88. Presiding in the Legislative Assembly

(1)   The Speaker, or in his or her absence the Deputy Speaker, shall preside over sittings of the Legislative Assembly.

(2)   In the absence from any sitting of both the Speaker and the Deputy Speaker, the members of the Legislative Assembly present shall choose one of their number (not being a Minister) to preside over that sitting.

(3)   The Speaker, or the Deputy Speaker, or any other member of the Legislative Assembly while presiding over a sitting of the Legislative Assembly in the absence of the Speaker and Deputy Speaker, shall –
    (a)   act in a strictly non-partisan manner, performing his or her functions impartially, in the service of the whole House; and
    (b)   ensure that in the conduct of the business of the Legislative Assembly there is an opportunity for all members present to be fairly heard.

89. Quorum

No business shall be transacted at any sitting of the Legislative Assembly if objection is taken by any member of the Legislative Assembly present that the number of members present is (besides the Speaker or other member presiding) fewer than one-half of the total number of members (excluding any vacancies).

90. Voting

(1)   Except as otherwise provided in this Constitution, every question in the Legislative Assembly shall be decided by a majority of the votes of the Members of Parliament present and voting.

(2)   The Speaker, or the Deputy Speaker, or any other member of the Legislative Assembly while presiding over a sitting of the Legislative Assembly in the absence of the Speaker and Deputy Speaker, shall not have a deliberative vote but, in the case of an equality of votes, shall have a casting vote.

91. Unqualified Persons Sitting or Voting

(1)   Any person who sits or votes in the Legislative Assembly knowing or having reasonable grounds for knowing that he or she is not entitled to do so shall be guilty of an offence and liable to a fine as prescribed by Act of Parliament for each day on which he or she so sits or votes.

(2)   Any prosecution for an offence under this section shall be instituted in the High Court and shall not be so instituted except by the Director of Public Prosecutions.

92. Validity of Proceedings

The Legislative Assembly may act notwithstanding any vacancy in its membership (including any vacancy not filled when the Assembly first meets after a general election) and the presence or participation of any person not entitled to be present at or to participate in the proceedings of the Assembly shall not invalidate those proceedings.

93. Introduction of Bills

(1)   Subject to subsection (2), any member of the Legislative Assembly may introduce any bill or propose any motion for debate in the Legislative Assembly, or present any petition to the Legislation Assembly, and the same shall be considered and disposed of by the Legislative Assembly under the provisions of the Standing Orders.

(2)   For the avoidance of doubt, any previously existing convention regarding the need to obtain the consent of the Crown before introducing bill no longer applies.

(3)   Except upon the recommendation of the President, signified by a Minister, the Legislative Assembly shall not proceed upon any bill or amendment to a bill which, in the opinion of the person presiding in the Legislative Assembly, would dispose of or charge the Consolidated Fund or any other public fund or account, or revoke or alter any disposition thereof or charge thereon, or impose, alter or repeal any tax, rate or duty.

94. Assent and Enactment of Legislation

(1)   The power of Parliament to make laws shall be exercised by bills passed by the Legislative Assembly and assented to by the President.

(2)   When a bill is submitted to the President for assent in accordance with the provisions of this Constitution he or she shall within seven days signify that he or she assents; and if the President fails to assent to the bill within seven days he or she shall be deemed to have assented to the bill on the expiration of that period.

(3)   When the President assents to a bill, or is deemed to have assented to a bill, that has been submitted to him or her in accordance with this Constitution, the bill shall become law and the President shall thereupon cause it to be published in the Gazette as law.

(4)   No law made by Parliament shall come into operation until it has been published in the Gazette but Parliament may postpone the coming into operation of any such law and may, subject to the provisions of section 12, make laws with retrospective effect.

(5)   The enacting formula for Acts of Parliament shall be, 'Be it enacted by the President of the Republic of Northumbria, by and with the advice and consent of the representatives of the people in Legislative Assembly convened, and by the authority of the same, as follows....'

95. Parliamentary Procedures

(1)   Subject to this Constitution, the Legislative Assembly may regulate its own procedure and may make Standing Orders and other rules for the orderly conduct of its own proceedings.

(2)   Parliament may, for the purpose of the orderly and
       effective discharge of business, make provision for the
       powers, privileges and immunities of the Legislative
       Assembly and the committees and members thereof;
       provided, that until such provision is made, the powers,
       privileges and immunities of the Legislative Assembly,
       its committees and members, shall, *mutatis mutandis,*
       be those of the House of Commons immediately before
       the appointed day.

(3)   Government business shall usually have priority in the
       Legislative Assembly, provided that –
       (a)   at least one-fifth of all sitting days in each session
              ('Opposition Days') shall be reserved for
              Opposition business, proportionally divided
              between the official Opposition and other
              opposition parties according to their number of
              members in the Legislative Assembly; and
       (b)   at least one-tenth of all sitting days in each
              session ('Backbench Days') shall be reserved for
              private members' and backbench business.

(4)   It shall be the duty of the Speaker, in consultation with
       the leaders of the political parties in the Legislative
       Assembly, to ensure the fair allocation of Opposition
       Days and Backbench Days throughout each session.

96. President's Address

       At the opening of each session of Parliament, the
       President shall address the Legislative Assembly, in
       terms prescribed by the Prime Minister, to set out the
       Government's policy priorities and legislative agenda
       for the forthcoming session; after the withdrawal of the

President, this speech shall be the subject of a vote in reply on a substantive motion, which shall be treated as a test of the Assembly's confidence in the Government.

97. Committees of the Legislative Assembly

(1)   The Legislative Assembly shall appoint from among its members -
   (a)   a Public Accounts Committee;
   (b)   a Committee of Standards and Privileges; and
   (c)   such other committees as may be required by Act of Parliament or by order of the Legislative Assembly.

(2)   A committee of the Legislative Assembly may, subject to his Constitution and to any other law-
   (a)   examine draft bills;
   (b)   review the enforcement of laws and propose measures for such enforcement;
   (c)   investigate or inquire into the activities or administration of any Ministry or public institution;
   (d)   require a Minister or any public officer it to provide the committee with information relating to their respective functions, and to answer questions, orally or in writing;
   (e)   perform any other function assigned to it by Act of Parliament or by order of the Legislative Assembly.

(3)   Parliament may confer on committees appointed under this section powers for compelling the production of documents, enforcing the attendance of witnesses, and examining them on oath, affirmation or otherwise.

(4) Committees of the Legislative Assembly shall be so composed as fairly to reflect the partisan and gender balance of the Legislative Assembly.

(5) The chairs of committees shall be elected by the Legislative Assembly, by secret ballot, in such a manner as to ensure that all parties have a proportional share of committee chair-ships; provided, that the chair of the Public Accounts Committee must be a member of the official Opposition in the Legislative Assembly.

(6) Except for the Committee of Standards and Privileges, or any administrative committee for the management of the staff, buildings and facilities of Parliament, no person holding ministerial office may be a member of any committee of the Legislative Assembly.

98. Proceedings to be Public

(1) Subject to subsection (2), the proceedings of the Legislative Assembly shall be held in public.

(2) The Legislative Assembly may, by a decision of a two-thirds majority of the members present, authorise a closed sitting of the Assembly, or of any committee, for the consideration of matters of national security.

(3) There shall be an official record of the proceedings of the Legislative Assembly which shall be published and made available to the public.

99. Remuneration of Members

(1) Members of the Legislative Assembly shall be entitled to such remuneration and allowances as may be determined by Act of Parliament.

(2) Until otherwise provided by Act of Parliament, the remuneration and allowances of members of the Legislative Assembly shall be the same as those payable to members of the House of Commons immediately before the appointed day.

(3) No bill for an Act of Parliament to alter the remuneration or allowances of the members of the Legislative Assembly shall come into effect until after a general election shall have been held.

100. Declarations of Interest

(1) There shall be a register of interests, in which the members of the Legislative Assembly must disclose their pecuniary interests, and which shall be published and made available for public inspection.

(2) Any member of the Legislative Assembly who has a financial interest (including benefits in kind) in any matter –
  (a) must declare that interest before taking part in any proceedings of the Legislative Assembly (as the case may be) or any committee relating to that matter; and
  (b) may not vote in the Legislative Assembly, or any committee on a question relating to that matter.

(3)   The Legislative Assembly shall make further provision
        by standing orders for the enforcement of this section,
        which may include the suspension from the Legislative
        Assembly of a member who fails to comply with, or
        acts in contravention to, subsections (1) or (2) or any
        provisions so made for the enforcement thereof.

Division IV. Summoning, Prorogation and Dissolution

101. Sessions of the Legislative Assembly

(1)   Subject to the provisions of this section, the Legislative
        Assembly shall meet at such times and at such places as
        the President, on the advice of the Prime Minister, from
        time to time appoints by proclamation.

(2)   Except if prevented by war, natural disaster, or other
        emergency, the Legislative Assembly shall normally
        meet in the City of York.

(3)   The Legislative Assembly shall meet not later than
        thirty days after the holding of a general election.

(4)   The Legislative Assembly shall hold at least one
        session in every year, arranged such that a period of
        four months shall not intervene between the last sitting
        of the Legislative Assembly in one session and the first
        sitting thereof in the next session.

(5)   The Legislative Assembly, if adjourned or prorogued,
        shall be summoned by the President to meet within ten
        days, if so advised by the Speaker on the request made

in writing of not less than one-third of the members of
the Legislative Assembly.

102. Prorogation of Legislative Assembly

(1)   Subject to subsection (2), the President, acting on the
advice of the Prime Minister, may at any time, by
proclamation, prorogue the Legislative Assembly.

(2)   The President shall not prorogue the Legislative
Assembly unless satisfied, in his or her discretion, that,
in tendering that advice, the Prime Minister commands
the confidence of a majority of the members of the
Legislative Assembly; and if not so satisfied, the
President may refuse to prorogue the Legislative
Assembly until such confidence is demonstrated.

103. Dissolution of Parliament

(1)   Subject to this section, the Legislative Assembly shall
continue for four years from the date of its first meeting
following the most recent general election; at the expiry
of that period the President shall dissolve Parliament.

(2)   If Northumbria is at war, or a state of public emergency
is in effect, the duration of the Legislative Assembly
may be extended, by means of a resolution passed by a
two-thirds majority of the members Legislative
Assembly, for a period of up to twelve months; this
may be further extended, for an additional period of up
to twelve months, by a resolution passed by a three-
fourths majority of the members of the Legislative
Assembly; and at the end of that period of extension,

Parliament shall be dissolved.

(3) The President may at any time dissolve Parliament on the advice of the Prime Minister; provided that the President may, at his or her own discretion, refuse to dissolve the Legislative Assembly if so advised by a Prime Minister who does not command the confidence of the Legislative Assembly and if it shall appear to the President that a Prime Minister can be appointed who could govern for a reasonable period with a working majority in the Assembly.

(4) If the Legislative Assembly passes a resolution of no confidence in the Government and the Prime Minister does not within five days of the passing of that resolution either resign from office or advise a dissolution, the President may at his or her own discretion dissolve Parliament.

(5) If the office of Prime Minister has been vacant for not less than thirty days, and the President is satisfied that there is no realistic prospect of being able within a reasonable time to appoint a Prime Minister who can command the confidence of a majority of the members of the Legislation Assembly, the President may, acting at his or her own discretion, dissolve Parliament.

104. General Elections

There shall be a general election of the Legislative Assembly at such time, within three months after the most recent dissolution of the Legislative Assembly, as the President, acting on the advice of the Chair of the

Electoral and Boundaries Commission, shall by proclamation appoint.

105. Emergency Session After Dissolution

(1)   If between a dissolution of the Legislative Assembly and the next ensuing general election to the Legislative Assembly, an emergency arises of such a nature that in the opinion of the Prime Minister, it is necessary for the Legislative Assembly to meet before the general election can be held, the President, on the advice of the Prime Minister, may summon the Legislative Assembly that has been dissolved; but the election of members of the Legislative Assembly shall proceed, subject to subsection (2) of section 103, and the Legislative Assembly that has been summoned shall, if not sooner dissolved, stand dissolved on the day on which the general election is held.

(2)   The provisions of subsection (5) of section 101 shall not apply when Parliament is dissolved.

Division V. Leader of the Opposition

106. Leader of the Opposition

(1)   There shall be a Leader of the Opposition who shall be appointed by the President.

(2)   Whenever there shall be occasion for the appointment of a Leader of the Opposition, the President shall appoint -

(a) if there is one opposition party whose number of seats in the Legislative Assembly is –
    (i) at least one-fourth of the total number of seats; and
    (ii) more than the number of seats of any other opposition party;
the member of the Legislative Assembly who is the recognised Leader in the Legislative Assembly of that party; or

(b) if, no person is qualified for appointment under paragraph (a) of this sub-section, the member of the Legislative Assembly who, in the judgment of the President after consultation with the Speaker, commands the support of the largest single group of members of the Legislative Assembly in opposition to the Government who are prepared to support one leader.

(3) The office of Leader of the Opposition shall become vacant -

(a) if after any dissolution of the Legislative Assembly, he or she is informed by the President that the President is about to appoint another person as Leader of the Opposition;

(b) if he or she ceases to be a member of the Legislative Assembly otherwise than by a dissolution; or

(c) if his or her appointment is revoked under the provisions of sub-section (4).

(4) If a member of the Legislative Assembly other than the Leader of the Opposition has become the Leader of the opposition party having the greatest numerical strength in the Legislative Assembly or, as the case may be, the Leader of the Opposition has ceased to command the

support of the largest single group of members in opposition to the Government, the President at his or her own discretion shall revoke the appointment of the Leader of the Opposition.

(5)   Sub-section (4) shall not have effect while the Legislative Assembly is dissolved.

(6)   The salary of the Leader of the Opposition shall be equal to that of a Cabinet Minister.

PART VII. DEFENCE AND INTERNATIONAL RELATIONS

107. Defence Service of Northumbria

(1)   There shall be a Defence Service of Northumbria, consisting of land, sea and air components.

(2)   The functions of the Defence Service may include –
    (a)   defence and protection of the sovereignty and territorial integrity of Northumbria;
    (b)   protection of Northumbria's airspace, territorial waters and exclusive economic zone;
    (c)   contribution to the collective defence and security of Northumbria's allies;
    (d)   participation in peace-support and humanitarian missions; and
    (e)   providing assistance to civil authorities in situations of emergency or disaster.

(3)   Parliament shall by law regulate the recruitment, organisation, discipline, pay and allowances, and administration of the Defence Service.

108. Supreme Command

(1)   The supreme command of the Defence Service of Northumbria shall be vested in the President.

(2)   The President shall exercise command only on the advice of the Prime Minister, or on the advice of the Minister of Defence acting under the general direction of the Prime Minister.

109. Defence Council

(1)   There shall be a Defence Council which shall –
   (a)   advise the Prime Minister on matters relating to defence, security and the Defence Service;
   (b)   be responsible, under the supervision of the Minister of Defence, for the overall policy, administration and control of the Defence Service; and
   (c)   perform any other functions related to defence, security and the Defence Service as may be prescribed by national legislation.

(2)   The Defence Council consist of-
   (a)   the Minister of Defence, as chairperson;
   (b)   the Chief of the Defence Service of Northumbria;
   (c)   the senior officers of the land, sea and air components;
   (d)   the Permanent Secretary in the Ministry of Defence;
   (e)   the senior officer responsible for defence logistics; and

(f)   such other persons as the Prime Minister, after consulting the Minister of Defence, may from time to time summon and appoint to the Defence Council.

provided, that the Prime Minister shall have the right to summon and attend meetings of the Defence Council, and that when present at its meetings the Prime Minister shall preside.

(3)   Further provisions on the composition, organization and functions of the Defence Council may be made by Act of Parliament, and, subject to any Act of Parliament, by the President on the advice of the Prime Minister.

110. Declaration of War

(1)   Subject to subsection (2), war shall not be declared, and Northumbria shall not participate in any armed conflict, except with the prior approval, by resolution, of the Legislative Assembly.

(2)   If the territory of Northumbria is invaded or attacked, or is at imminent risk of being invaded or attacked, or if Northumbria is bound by a collective defence alliance to come to the aid of any ally who has been, or is at imminent risk of being, invaded or attacked, the President acting on the advice of the Prime Minister may undertake such immediate defensive action as the Prime Minister shall deem necessary; and the Prime Minister shall, as soon as may be practicable thereafter, make a statement to the Legislative Assembly requesting retrospective approval.

111. Promotion of International Peace and Security

The Republic shall base its international relations on the principles of respect for national sovereignty and equality, non-interference in the internal affairs of other countries, peaceful settlement of international disputes, and respect for international law and the principles of the Commonwealth Charter and the United Nations Charter.

112. International Treaties

(1) The President, acting on the advice of the Prime Minister or of the Minister for Foreign Affairs acting under the general direction of the Prime Minister, may ratify treaties, conventions and agreements (whosoever designated) with foreign countries or international organisations.

(2) All treaties, conventions and agreements, before being ratified, shall be communicated to the Legislative Assembly by ministerial statement and laid before the Legislative Assembly for a period of at least twenty-one days.

(3) A treaty, convention or agreement shall not be ratified if within the period specified by subsection (2) the Legislative Assembly by resolution votes against its ratification.

(4) No treaty, convention or agreement shall have effect as part of the law of Northumbria unless adopted into Northumbrian law by or in accordance with an Act of Parliament.

PART VIII. THE JUDICIARY

113. Judicial Authorities

(1)   The judicial authority of Northumbria shall be vested in
-

    (a)   the Supreme Court of Northumbria;

    (b)   the Court of Appeal;

    (c)   the High Court;

    (d)   the Criminal Court (formerly known as the Crown Court);

    (e)   such courts and tribunals as may from time to time be established in and for Northumbria, or any part thereof, by Act of Parliament.

(2)   Subject to this Constitution, the courts and tribunals shall have such composition as may be prescribed by law and shall have such jurisdiction, powers and authority as may be conferred upon them by law.

(3)   Until otherwise provided by law in accordance with this Constitution, the composition, jurisdiction, powers and authority of all courts in Northumbria shall remain as they were immediately before the appointed day.

114. Supreme Court of Northumbria

(1)   The Supreme Court of Northumbria shall consist of –

    (a)   the Chief Justice of Northumbria,

    (b)   at least four but not more than eleven Associate Justices.

(2) In addition to any other jurisdiction conferred upon it by any Act of Parliament, the Supreme Court of Northumbria shall have final appellate authority over any case concerning -

(a) any question as to the interpretation, operation or application of this Constitution, including questions as to the compatibility with this Constitution of any Act of Parliament, or any other instrument having the force of law;

(b) the enforcement of constitutionally protected fundamental rights and liberties; or

(c) a question of law of general public interest.

(3) Notwithstanding anything in this section, the Supreme Court may, in its discretion, grant special leave to appeal from any judgment, decree, determination, sentence or order in any cause or matter passed or made by any court or tribunal in Northumbria.

(4) An Act of Parliament may confer upon the Supreme Court such supplemental powers not inconsistent with any of the provisions of this Constitution as may appear to be necessary or desirable for the purpose of enabling the Court more effectively to exercise the jurisdiction conferred upon it by or under this Constitution.

(5) If at any time it appears to the Attorney-General that a question of law has arisen, or is likely to arise, which is of such a nature and of such public importance that it is expedient to obtain the opinion of the Supreme Court upon it, he or she may refer the question to the Supreme Court for consideration and the Supreme Court may, after such hearing as it thinks fit, report its opinion thereon.

(6)   The Supreme Court shall have power to issue directions, orders or writs, including writs of habeas corpus, quashing orders, mandatory orders and prohibiting orders, as required for the enforcement of this Constitution and the protection of constitutional rights and liberties.

(7)   All courts in Northumbria shall be bound to follow the decisions of the Supreme Court on questions of law.

115. Appointment of Judges

(1)   All judges of the courts established by or in accordance with subsection (1) of section 113 shall be appointed by the President on the advice of the Judicial Service Commission established by section 116.

(2)   The transfer or promotion of a judge shall be considered to be a new appointment and this section shall be applied accordingly.

(3)   No person shall be appointed to any judicial office unless he or she possesses such legal qualifications and has such experience in legal practice, or previous service in judicial office, as may be prescribed by Act of Parliament; or, subject to any Act of Parliament, by the Judicial Service Commission.

(4)   In making recommendations for judicial appointments the Judicial Service Commission shall –
    (a)   recommend candidates for appointment solely on merit, according to their legal expertise and experience, as well as their personal integrity and suitability of character; and

(b)   subject to paragraph (a), ensure that, as far as may be practicable, the judiciary reflects, and is inclusive of, Northumbrian society with respect to the gender, ethnicity, religion and socio-economic class.

116. Judicial Service Commission

(1)   The Judicial Service Commission shall consist of –

    (a)   four members ('lay members'), one who whom shall be Chairperson of the Commission, appointed under subsection (2),

    (b)   three members ('judicial members'), one of whom shall be Deputy Chairperson of the Commission, appointed under subsection (3), and

    (c)   two members ('legal members') appointed under subsection (4).

(2)   The lay members shall be appointed by the President on the advice of the Prime Minister given with the concurrence of the Leader of Opposition, from amongst persons who are not, and have never been, qualified legal practitioners, in order to represent the general public interest.

(3)   The judicial members shall be appointed by the President on the advice of the Chief Justice of the Supreme Court, given after consulting the Associate Justices of the Supreme Court, from amongst those who have held judicial office for at least three years.

(4)   The legal members shall be appointed by the President on the advice of the Chairperson of the Judicial Service Commission, given after consultation with the

organisations recognised by law as representative of legal professionals, from amongst members of the legal professions.

(5)   A person shall not be qualified to be appointed to the Judicial Service Commission if he or she is, or at any time in the five years immediately preceding his or her appointment has been —

    (a)   a member of the Legislative Assembly or any local authority;

    (b)   nominated as a candidate for election as a member of the Legislative Assembly or any local authority.

    (c)   the holder of an office in, or the employee of, any registered political party.

(6)   A member of the Judicial Service Commission shall cease to hold office—

    (a)   if he or she submits his or her resignation in writing to the President;

    (b)   if any circumstances arise that, if he or she were not a member of a Judicial Service Commission, would cause him or her to be disqualified to be appointed to that office; or

    (c)   if he or she is removed from office in accordance with subsection (7).

    (d)   at the expiration of four years from the date of his or her appointment.

(7)   A member of the Judicial Service Commission may not be removed from office during his or her term except by means of a resolution calling for removal on the grounds of incapacity, neglect of duty, or gross misconduct passed by a two-thirds majority of the members of the Legislative Assembly.

(8)   In the event of the death, resignation, or removal of any of a member of the Judicial Service Commission, the vacancy shall be filled as soon as may be practicable in accordance with this section.

(9)   The Judicial Service Commission may continue to perform its functions notwithstanding any vacancy in its membership or the absence of any member: provided that any decisions of the Commission shall require the concurrence of a majority of all its members.

(10)   The Judicial Service Commission may regulate its own procedure and shall not be subject to the direction or control of any other person or authority.

117. Tenure and Removal of Judges

(1)   Subject to the provisions of this section, a member of the judiciary shall vacate his or her office when he or she attains the retirement age prescribed by law, but the retirement age applicable to any member of the judiciary shall not be altered after his or her appointment, except with his or her consent.

(2)   A member of the judiciary may resign from office by writing under his or her hand addressed to the President, who on receipt of such resignation shall inform the Judicial Service Commission accordingly.

(3)   A member of the judiciary shall not be removed from office except by means of a resolution of the Legislative Assembly supported by the votes of not less

than two-thirds of its membership; and no such resolution shall be passed by the Legislative Assembly unless the Judicial Service Commission has conducted an independent enquiry into the conduct or capacity of the judge, and has recommended to the Legislative Assembly, based on the findings of that enquiry, that the judge ought to be removed on the grounds of misbehaviour, incapacity or neglect of duty.

(4)   No discussion shall take place in the Legislative Assembly with respect to the conduct of any member of the judiciary in the discharge of his or her judicial duties except upon a motion for removal under the terms of this section.

(5)   A judicial office shall not be abolished while there is a substantive office holder.

118. Judicial Independence and Neutrality

(1)   The courts and tribunals, and all judges and magistrates, are independent of the legislative and executive branches of Government, and shall be subject only to this Constitution and the law.

(2)   All persons with responsibility for matters relating to the judiciary or to the administration of justice must uphold the continued independence of the judiciary and must not seek to influence particular judicial decisions through any special access to the judiciary.

(3)   A person holding office as a judge or magistrate shall not –

(a)   be a member of, a candidate for election to, the
       Legislative Assembly or any local authority;
(b)   be an active member of, or reported donor to, any
       political party, or
(c)   act in such a way as to call his or her political
       neutrality into question.

119. Oaths of Judges

A judge shall not enter upon the duties of his or her
office unless he or she has taken and subscribed the
Oath of Allegiance and the Judicial Oath in the forms
set out in the First Schedule.

PART IX. THE PUBLIC SERVICE

120. The Public Service

(1)   There shall be a Public Service of Northumbria, which
       shall be established as a permanent, professional and
       non-partisan civil service for the administration of
       Northumbria under the direction of responsible
       Ministers.

(2)   The Public Service does not include service in any of
       the following capacities –
       (a)   President;
       (b)   Prime Minister or a Minister, including the
              Attorney-General;
       (c)   Speaker, Deputy Speaker, or other Member of
              the Legislative Assembly;

(d)   Chief Justice or Justice of the Supreme Court or any other member of the judiciary;

(e)   a member, officer or employee of any local authority;

(f)   a police officer; or

(g)   a member of any uniformed branch of the Defence Service;

(h)   any unpaid honorary office of a ceremonial nature; or

(i)   any office to which section 125 applies.

(3)   Following offices shall not be offices in the Public Service, but are offices to which Public Officers may be seconded, or which may be held by Public Officers under the terms of sub-section (5) of section 134 –

(a)   the Clerk of the Legislative Assembly, and the other officers of Parliament;

(b)   Ombudsman;

(c)   Auditor-General;

(d)   the Chairperson and other members of –
   (i)   the Human Rights Commission,
   (ii)   the Judicial Service Commission,
   (iii)   the Public Service Commission,
   (iv)   the Electoral and Boundaries Commission.

121. Public Service Commission

(1)   There shall be a Public Service Commission of Northumbria, which shall consist of a Chair of the Commission and four other Commissioners, appointed by the President, acting on the advice of the Prime Minister given with the concurrence of the Leader of the Opposition.

(2)   No person shall be appointed to be a member of the
       Public Service Commission if he or she –
       (a)   is not a citizen of Northumbria;
       (b)   is, or has within the period of five years
              immediately preceding his or her appointment
              been, a Member of, or candidate for election to,
              the Legislative Assembly or any local authority;
       (c)   is an active member of, or reported donor to, any
              political party.

(3)   At least two members of the Public Service
       Commission shall be appointed from amongst persons
       who are suitably qualified and experienced in the senior
       management of public sector or non-profit institutions.

(4)   At least one member of the Public Service Commission
       shall be appointed after consultation with the unions or
       professional associations recognised as representing the
       interests of members of the Public Service.

(5)   If a member of the Public Service is appointed to the
       Public Service Commission, he or she shall not, while
       continuing as a member of the Public Service
       Commission, hold any other office or exercise any
       other function in the Public Service.

(6)   The powers of the Public Service Commission shall not
       be affected by any vacancy in the number of its
       members, and any proceedings of the Public Service
       Commission shall be valid notwithstanding that some
       person who was not entitled to do so took part in those
       proceedings.

122. Term of office

(1) A member of the Public Service Commission shall be appointed to hold office for a term of five years and shall, if otherwise qualified and not disqualified, be eligible for reappointment.

(2) A member of the Public Service Commission may at any time resign his or her office by writing under his or her hand addressed to the President.

(3) A member of the Public Service Commission shall cease to hold office as such if he or she ceases to be qualified, or becomes disqualified, under the provisions of subsection (2) of section 121.

(4) Except as provided in subsection (3), a member of the Public Service Commission shall not be removed from office except by means of a resolution of the Legislative Assembly supported by the votes of not less than two-thirds of its membership, on grounds of misbehaviour, incapacity or neglect of duty.

123. Functions of the Commission

(1) The Public Service Commission shall be responsible for ensuring the integrity, impartiality, professionalism of the public service and shall exercise the functions conferred by this section with the object of maintaining the principle of equal opportunities, and selection and promotion on merit, in relation to public appointments.

(2) Subject to this Constitution, and in accordance with any rules prescribed by or according to law, the Public

Service Commission shall have the power to recruit, select and appoint all public officers, except those to which sections 124 or 125 apply, including the power to –

(a)   make appointments by promotion and transfer,

(b)   confirm acting or temporary appointments, and

(c)   remove and otherwise exercise lawful disciplinary control over public officers.

(3)   Subject to this Constitution, and in accordance with any rules prescribed by or according to law, the Public Service Commission may delegate the exercise any of its functions under subsection (2) to designated 'appointing authorities', which may include the following –

(a)   a Minister;

(b)   the Chairperson or any member of the Public Service Commission, or committee thereof;

(c)   the Cabinet Secretary;

(c)   the Permanent Secretary of any Department; or

(d)   with the approval of the Permanent Secretary of the Department concerned, any public officer in that Department.

(4)   Subject to this Constitution, and in accordance with any rules prescribed by or according to law, the Public Service Commission –

(a)   shall prescribe and publish a Code of Practice on the interpretation and application by the appointing authorities of the principles specified in subsection (1);

(b)   may adopt and publish from time to time such additional guidance to appointing authorities as the Public Service shall think fit;

(c)   shall audit public appointment policies and practices pursued by appointing authorities to establish whether the Code of Practice is being observed by appointing authorities;

(d)   may require appointing authorities to publish such summary information as may be specified relating to selection for public appointment; and

(e)   may conduct an inquiry into the policies and practices followed by an appointing authority in relation to any public appointment or disciplinary process.

(5)   Subject to this Constitution, and in accordance with any rules prescribed by or according to law, the Public Service Commission may regulate its own procedure and determine its own order of business.

(6)   The Public Service Commission shall make an annual report on its activities to the President, who shall without delay cause a copy of that report to be laid before the Legislative Assembly.

(7)   Additional powers and functions, related to the regulation and management of the Public Service, may be vested in the Public Service Commission by or under Acts of Parliament.

124. Prime Ministerial Approval of Senior Appointments

(1)   This section applies to the offices of –
   (a)   Secretary to the Cabinet;
   (b)   Permanent Secretary of a Department and other public officers of equivalent rank; and

(c)   Ambassador, High Commissioner, or other
        principal representative of Northumbria in
        another country or to any international
        organisation of which Northumbria is a member.

(2)   The power to appoint persons to hold or to act in offices
       to which this section applies (including the power to
       confirm appointments), and the power to exercise
       disciplinary control over persons holding or acting in
       such offices and the power to remove such persons
       from office shall vest in the President on the advice of
       the Chairperson of the Public Service Commission
       given with the concurrence of the Prime Minister; and
       if the Prime Minister objects in writing to any candidate
       for appointment to an office to which this section
       applies, the Prime Minister may require the Public
       Service Commission to propose another candidate.

125. Appointment to Public Corporations etc.

(1)   This section applies to –
       (a)   directors, governors, board members, trustees,
               councillors, and other persons (howsoever
               designated) being members of, or having
               direction or supervisory control over, any
               publicly owned corporation, non-departmental
               public body or other statutory body;
       (b)   special advisors to Ministers; and
       (c)   all other public appointments, not being part of
               the Public Service or the Defence Service, whose
               appointment is not otherwise provided for by Act
               of Parliament.

(2)   The power to appoint persons to hold or to act in offices
        to which this section applies (including the power to
        confirm appointments), and the power to exercise
        disciplinary control over persons holding or acting in
        such offices and the power to remove such persons
        from office, shall, unless otherwise provided by Act of
        Parliament, vest in a responsible Minister.

(3)   A Minister exercising any power under this section
        shall act –
        (a)   in accordance with the principles of merit,
                fairness and openness;
        (b)   subject to the Code of Practice issued by the
                Public Service Commission; and
        (c)   subject to any requirement provided by law
                requiring the Minister to –
                (i)   appoint persons only having prescribed
                        qualifications or experience;
                (ii)   act after consultation with any other
                        person, authority or other body.

126. Public Service Board of Appeal

(1)   There shall be a Public Service Board of Appeal, which
        shall consist of:
        (a)   a judge of the Supreme Court, appointed by the
                President on the advice of the Chief Justice, who
                shall be the Chairperson of the Public Service
                Board of Appeal;
        (b)   one person appointed by the President, on the
                advice of the Prime Minister with the
                concurrence of the Leader of the Opposition; and
        (c)   one person, being an officer of the Public
                Service, elected by the officers of the Public

Service and holding office for a term not exceeding three years.

(2) An Act of Parliament may –

    (a)   make further provision by law for the qualification, composition, appointment and tenure of the members of the Public Service Board of Appeal, including –

        (i)   prescribing the manner of election of the person to be elected under the provisions of paragraph (c) of subsection (1); and

        (ii)   providing for the appointment of deputies to act for members of the Public Service Board of Appeal in the event of absence or incapacity.

    (b)   determine the remuneration of members of the Public Service Board of Appeal; and

    (c)   prescribe the jurisdiction of the Board of Appeal to hear and determine appeals from decisions about human resource management matters in the Public Service.

127. Ombudsman

(1) There shall be an Ombudsman who shall be appointed by the President on the advice of the Public Service Commission.

(2) The appointment of the Ombudsman shall be made on merit, pursuant to any selection and appointment criteria and other terms and conditions as may be provided by Act of Parliament.

(3)   The Ombudsman shall serve for a term of six years and shall continue to hold office, subject to subsections (4) and (5), until his or her successor is appointed.

(4)   The Ombudsman may resign from office by submitting his or her resignation in writing to the President.

(5)   The Ombudsman may be removed from office only by means of a resolution passed by a two-thirds majority of the members of the Legislative Assembly praying for his or her removal on grounds of incapacity, neglect of duty, or gross misconduct.

128. Functions of Ombudsman

(1)   The principal functions of the Ombudsman shall be to provide citizens with a means of redress against maladministration, to prevent and rectify arbitrary or unfair administrative decisions, to promote good governance, and to make recommendations for the improvement of the practices and procedures of public bodies.

(2)   The Ombudsman shall have the authority –
  (a)   to enquire into the conduct of any person to whom this section applies in the exercise of his or her office or authority; and
  (b)   to enquire into any decision or recommendation made, including any advice given or recommendation made to a Minister, or any act done or omitted by any department of Government or any other authority to which this section applies, or by officers or members of such a department or authority, being action

taken in exercise of the administrative functions of that department or authority.

(3) The Ombudsman may conduct enquires in the following circumstances –

    (a) where a complaint is duly made to the Ombudsman by any person alleging that the complainant has sustained an injustice as a result of a fault in administration;

    (b) where a member of the Legislative Assembly requests the Ombudsman to investigate the matter on the ground that a person or body of persons specified in the request has or may have sustained such injustice; or

    (c) in any other circumstances in which the Ombudsman considers that he or she ought to investigate the matter on the ground that some person or body of persons has or may have sustained such injustice.

(4) Subject to subsection (5), the Ombudsman's investigatory authority shall extend to –

    (a) all departments, ministries and agencies of the Government of Northumbria;

    (b) all offices, commissions, corporate bodies and public agencies established by or under any Act of Parliament;

    (c) all local authorities;

    (d) all private persons, businesses or corporations acting on behalf of, or under contract with, the Government or any department, ministry or agency thereof, or any regional or local authority, in so far as it relates to their contractual obligations for the provision, distribution or management of goods or services for or on behalf of the public.

(5) The Ombudsman's investigatory authority shall not extend to –
(a) the President;
(b) any judge or magistrate in the exercise of his or her judicial functions; or
(c) except as otherwise provided by Act of Parliament, the Defence Service.

(6) In determining whether to initiate, continue or discontinue an enquiry, the Ombudsman shall act in his or her discretion and, in particular and without prejudice to the generality of this discretion, the Ombudsman may refuse to initiate or may discontinue an enquiry where it appears to him or her that –
(a) the subject matter of the complaint is trivial;
(b) the complaint is frivolous, vexatious, or not made in good faith; or
(c) the complainant has not a sufficient interest in the substance of the complaint.

(7) Where in the course of an enquiry it appears to the Ombudsman that there is evidence of any corrupt act by any public officer or by any other person in connection with the public service, the Ombudsman shall report the matter to the appropriate authority with his or her recommendation as to any further investigation he or she may consider proper.

(8) The Ombudsman shall make an annual report and may make such additional reports to the Legislative Assembly as he or she deems appropriate concerning the discharge of his or her functions, and may draw

attention to any defects which appear to him or her to exist in the administration or in any law.

(9) Parliament may by law confer additional functions on the Ombudsman and may make provision for regulating the procedure for the making of complaints and requests to the Ombudsman and for the exercise of his or her functions.

(10) Where after making an enquiry the Ombudsman is of the opinion that the action that was the subject-matter of enquiry was contrary to law, based wholly or partly on a mistake of law or fact, unreasonably delayed, or otherwise unjust or manifestly unreasonable the Ombudsman shall –
   (a) report his or her opinion, and his or her reasons, to the principal officer of any department or authority concerned, or other authority responsible for the action, and may make such recommendations as he or she thinks fit, and
   (b) request that officer to notify him, within a specified time, of any steps that it is proposed to take to give effect to such recommendations.

(11) Where after a report under subsection (10) is submitted no action is taken which seems to the Ombudsman to be adequate and appropriate within such period as the Ombudsman may prescribe, the Ombudsman, if he or she thinks fit, after considering any comments made by or on behalf of any department, authority, body or person affected, may send a copy of the report and recommendations to the Prime Minister and to any Minister concerned, and may thereafter make such further report to the Legislative Assembly on the matter as he or she thinks fit.

PART X. FINANCE

129. Public Funds and Revenues

(1)   There shall be a Consolidated Fund of Northumbria and such other public funds or accounts as may be provided by Act of Parliament.

(2)   No tax, charge, custom, duty, or other revenue, shall be imposed except by or under the authority of an Act of Parliament.

(3)   All taxes and other revenues and money raised or received by Northumbria shall be paid into the Consolidated Fund unless required or permitted by Act of Parliament to be paid into any other public fund or account.

130. Withdrawals from Public Funds

(1)   No monies shall be withdrawn from the Consolidated Fund except-
    (a)   to meet expenditure that is charged upon the Fund by this Constitution or by any Act of Parliament; or
    (b)   where the issue of those monies has been authorised by an appropriation law or by a law made in pursuance of section 132 of this Constitution.

(2)   Where any monies are charged by this Constitution or any Act of Parliament upon the Consolidated Fund or

any other public fund, they shall be paid out of that fund by the Government to the person or authority to whom payment is due.

(3)   No monies shall be withdrawn from any public fund other than the Consolidated Fund unless the issue of those monies has been authorised by or under an Act of Parliament.

(4)   There shall be such provision as may be made by Parliament prescribing the manner in which withdrawals may be made from the Consolidated Fund or any other public fund.

(5)   The investment of monies forming part of the Consolidated Fund shall be made in such a manner as may be prescribed by or under an Act of Parliament.

(6)   Notwithstanding the provision of subsection (1) of this section, provision may be made by or under an Act of Parliament authorising withdrawals to be made from the Consolidated Fund, in such circumstances and to such extent as may be prescribed by or under an Act of Parliament, for the purpose of making repayable advances.

131. Appropriation of Expenditures

(1)   The Minister responsible for finance shall, in respect of every financial year, cause to be laid before the Legislative Assembly a statement of the estimated receipts and expenditure for that year, and, unless Parliament in respect of any year otherwise provides,

that statement shall be so laid before the commencement of that year.

(2)   The proposals for all expenditure contained in the estimates (other than statutory expenditure) shall be submitted to the vote of the Legislative Assembly by means of an Appropriation Bill.

(3)   If, in respect of any financial year, it is found –
    (a)   that any expenditure is incurred or is likely to be incurred upon any service which is in excess of the sum provided for that service by the Appropriation Act relating to that year; or
    (b)   that any expenditure (other than statutory expenditure) is incurred or is likely to be incurred upon any service not provided for by the Appropriation Act relating to that year;
the Minister responsible for Finance shall cause to be laid before the Legislative Assembly supplementary estimates in respect of that expenditure, and the proposals for expenditure therein contained shall be submitted to the vote of the Assembly by means of a Supplementary Appropriation Bill.

(4)   Statutory expenditure, which shall not be submitted to the vote of the Legislative Assembly under the provisions of this section, means
    (a)   the expenditure charged on the Consolidated Fund by this Constitution.
    (b)   such other expenditure as may by Act of Parliament be charged upon the Consolidated Fund or any other public fund or account and in such Act be expressly stated to be statutory expenditure.

(5)   The Legislative Assembly may approve or refuse its
        approval to any proposal for expenditure contained in
        an Appropriation or Supplementary Appropriation Bill,
        but may not increase the amount or alter the destination
        of any proposed expenditure.

132. Expenditures in Advance of Appropriation

Parliament may make provision by law under which, if
the Appropriation Act in respect of any financial year
has not come into operation by the beginning of that
financial year, the Minister for the time being
responsible for Finance may authorize the withdrawal
of moneys from the Consolidated Fund for the purpose
of meeting expenditure necessary to carry on the
services of the Government of Northumbria until the
expiration of four months from the beginning of that
financial year or the coming into operation of the law,
whichever is the earlier.

133. Contingencies Fund

(1)   Parliament may make provision by law for the
        establishment of a Contingencies Fund and for
        authorising the Minister for the time being responsible
        for Finance, if satisfied that there has arisen an urgent
        and unforeseen need for expenditure for which no other
        suitable provision exists, to make advances from the
        Contingencies Fund to meet that need.

(2)   Where any advance is made from the contingencies
        Fund, a supplementary estimate shall as soon as
        possible be laid before the Legislative Assembly and

when the supplementary estimate has been approved by the Legislative Assembly, a supplementary Appropriation bill shall be introduced as soon as possible in the Legislative Assembly for the purpose of replacing the amount so advanced.

134. Remuneration of Judges and Constitutional Officers

(1)   This section applies to –
    (a)   all persons holding judicial office
    (b)   the Chairperson and other members of –
        (i)   the Human Rights Commission,
        (ii)   the Judicial Service Commissions,
        (iii)   the Public Service Commission,
        (iv)   the Electoral and Boundaries Commission.
    (c)   the Ombudsman;
    (d)   the Auditor-General;
    (e)   Permanent Secretaries; and
    (f)   the Secretary to the Cabinet.

(2)   Subject to subsection (3), the persons to which this section applies shall receive such salaries and allowances and shall be subject to such other terms and conditions of service as may from time to time be prescribed by Act of Parliament.

(3)   The salary and allowances payable to any person to which this section applies, and his or her terms and constitutions of service, shall not be altered to his or her disadvantage after his or her appointment.

(4)   The salary and allowances payable to any person to which this section applies shall be a charge upon the Consolidated Fund.

(5)   A person who was an officer or employee in the Public
        Service and who is appointed to an office under
        paragraphs (b), (c) or (d) of subsection (1), is entitled to
        retain all existing and accruing rights, including
        pension and seniority rights, as if the service of that
        person were a continuation of service as an officer or
        employee in the Public Service; and on ceasing to hold
        that office such person shall, unless removed on
        grounds of misconduct, have the right to return to the
        Public Service in their previous grade and with the
        seniority accrued while in that office.

135. Public Debt

(1)   All debt charges for which Northumbria is liable shall
        be a charge on the Consolidated Fund.

(2)   For the purposes of this section debt charges include
        interest, sinking fund charges, the repayment or
        amortization of debt and all expenditure in connection
        with the raising of loans on the security of the
        Consolidated Fund and the service and redemption of
        the debt created thereby.

136. Auditor General

(1)   There shall be an Auditor-General who shall be
        appointed by the President on the advice of the Public
        Service Commission.

(2)   The appointment of the Auditor-General shall be made
        on merit, pursuant to any selection and appointment

criteria and other terms and conditions as may be provided by Act of Parliament.

(3)   The Auditor-General shall serve for a term of six years and shall continue to hold office, subject to subsections (4) and (5), until his or her successor is appointed.

(4)   The Auditor-General may resign from office by submitting his or her resignation in writing to the President.

(5)   The Auditor-General may be removed from office only by means of a resolution passed by a two-thirds majority of the members of the Legislative Assembly praying for his or her removal on grounds of incapacity, neglect of duty, or gross misconduct.

137. Responsibilities of Auditor General

(1)   The Auditor-General shall have overall charge and direction of the National Audit Office, which shall have the authority audit and report upon the accounts of the Government, local authorities, and statutory public bodies.

(2)   The Auditor-General and any person authorised by him or her for the purpose of carrying out audits or inspections shall have access to all accounts, records, books, vouchers, documents, cash, stamps, securities, stores or other government property in the possession of any person in the service of a public authority.

(3)   For the purpose of exercising functions under this section, the Auditor General shall have such other

functions, powers, immunities and independence as may be vested in him or her by or in accordance with any Act of Parliament.

(4)   In the performance of his or her functions the Auditor General shall not be subject to the direction or control of any other person or authority.

(5)   The Auditor General shall make an annual report and may make such additional reports to the Legislative Assembly as he or she deems appropriate concerning the discharge of his or her functions, and may draw attention to any irregularities in the accounts, transactions, processes, systems or operations of the Consolidated Fund or of a public fund, account, Ministry, office or body audited by the Auditor General, and to any waste, inefficiency, or misuse of public funds.

138. Deputy Auditor General

(1)   There shall be a Deputy Auditor General, who shall be a senior public officer of the National Audit Office, and who shall advise, assist and deputise for the Auditor-General as required.

(2)   If the Auditor General is unable to carry out his or her functions because of illness, absence on leave, or any other reason, those functions shall be carried out by the Deputy Auditor General; and all powers and duties vested in the Auditor General by this Constitution or any law shall for the time being be delegated to the Deputy Auditor General for this purpose.

PART XI. LOCAL GOVERNMENT

139. Establishment of Local Government

(1)   For the purposes of decentralised local government, Northumbria shall be divided into such number of local authority areas, at parish, district, borough, city, county and regional levels, as may be determined by Act of Parliament.

(2)   No bill to abolish, merge, or alter the boundaries of, any existing local authority, shall be introduced to the Legislative Assembly unless each local authority to be affected by the proposed change has been consulted; and if any local authority by an absolute majority of its members objects to the proposed change, the bill shall not be deemed to have been passed by the Legislative Assembly unless approved by a two-thirds majority of the members thereof.

140. Powers and Functions of Local Government

(1)   The purposes of decentralised local government shall include –
   (a)   providing a forum for the representation of the locality;
   (b)   encouraging and assisting effective participation in public affairs;
   (c)   providing public services and facilities to the locality;
   (d)   managing and stewarding the resources of the locality;

(e)   promoting the wellbeing of the locality and wider public; and

(f)   performing such regulatory and administrative duties, and exercising such powers, as may be conferred on local authorities by law.

(2)   Subject to this Constitution, local authorities shall have such powers and functions as may, for the purposes specified in subsection (1), be vested in them by or under any Act of Parliament.

(3)   Unless otherwise prohibited by Act of Parliament, each local authority shall, for the purposes specified in subsection (1) have the power to do anything that a legal person may lawfully do.

(4)   Parliament shall, by law, confer powers on the local authorities to impose taxes for local purposes, to charge fees and receive fines, to set their budgets and to maintain funds.

141. Local Government Elections

(1)   Each local authority shall be under the direction of a council, the members of which shall be elected by the enfranchised voters resident in the locality, by proportional representation, as prescribed by Act of Parliament.

(2)   Each local council shall elect its own chairperson from amongst its members and shall designate one of its members, other than the chairperson, to act as leader of the council.

(3)   Notwithstanding subsections (1) and (2), provision may
       be made by Act of Parliament for the direct election of
       a mayor in any local authority, who shall be the chief
       executive of the local council, and for the direct
       election of other local officers whose powers are
       prescribed by law.

(4)   Except when a State of Emergency is in effect,
       elections to each local authority shall take place not
       later than the end of the fourth year after the year in
       which they were last held, and casual vacancies in the
       membership of local authorities shall be filled in
       accordance with law.

PART XII. ELECTIONS AND REFERENDUMS

142. Conduct of Elections and Referendums

(1)   In a referendum or an election to the Legislative
       Assembly or any local authority, the votes shall be
       given by secret ballot, but provision may be made by
       law for postal or proxy voting in the case of persons for
       who are unable to cast a ballot in person or unable
       without unreasonable inconvenience to attend a polling
       place.

(2)   Persons shall be registered to vote only in the
       constituency or ward in which they usually reside; or,
       in the case of citizens not currently resident in
       Northumbria, in the constituency or ward area in which
       they usually resided immediately before taking up
       residence outside of Northumbria.

(3)   Subject to this Constitution, additional provision may be made by Act of Parliament for the registration of voters, the conduct of elections, nomination of candidates, appointment of returning officers, election deposits, the regulation and registration of political parties, spending limits in campaigns, restrictions on sources of financing, reporting of donors and requirements to declare sources of financing, the suppression of corrupt or illicit electoral practices, and for any other purpose connected with the holding of elections and referendums.

(4)   Any law enacted under subsection (3), administrative rules, instructions, code of practice, or official guidance, issued under such law –
    (a)   must have as its purpose the promotion of free, fair and clean elections; and
    (b)   must not be designed to unfairly advantage or disadvantage any particular candidate or party.

(5)   A bill for an Act of Parliament under subsection (3) shall be submitted to the Electoral and Boundaries Commission for comment between its first and second readings in the Legislative Council, and the bill shall not proceed to its second reading unless the Electoral and Boundaries Commission has had a period of at least ninety days during which to study the bill and to report its analysis of the bill to the Legislative Assembly.

143. Electoral and Boundaries Commission

(1)   There shall be an Electoral and Boundaries Commission which shall consist of –

(a) three Commissioners, one of whom shall be the Chair of the Commission, to be appointed by the President on the advice of the Public Service Commission;

(b) two Commissioners appointed by the President on the advice of the Prime Minister;

(c) two Commissioners appointed by the President on the advice of the Leader of the Opposition; and

(d) two Commissioners appointed by the President on the advice of the Speaker of the Legislative Assembly, after consultation with the leaders of any parties represented in the Legislative Assembly other than the parties of the Prime Minister and the Leader of the Opposition.

(2) Of the three Commissioners appointed under paragraph (a) of subsection (1) –

(a) at least one shall be a serving or retired judge; and

(b) at least one shall be a serving or retired senior Public Officer with experience of electoral administration.

(3) A person shall not be qualified to be appointed to the Electoral and Boundaries Commission if he or she —

(a) is, or has at any time during the five years immediately preceding his appointment been, a member of the Legislative Assembly or any local authority;

(b) is, or has at any time during the said five years been, nominated as a candidate for election as a member of the Legislative Assembly or any local authority; or

(c)   is, or has at any time during the said five years been, the holder of an office in, or the employee of, or a reported donor to, any registered political party.

(4)   A member of the Electoral and Boundaries Commission shall not enter upon the duties of his or her office until he or she has taken and subscribed the Oath of Allegiance and the Oath of Office in the forms set out in the First Schedule.

(5)   A member of the Electoral and Boundaries Commission shall cease to hold office—
(a)   if he or she submits his resignation in writing to the President;
(b)   if any circumstances arise that, if he were not a member of the Commission, would cause him or her to be disqualified to be appointed as such;
(c)   if he or she is removed from office in accordance with subsection (6); or
(d)   at the expiration of six years from the date of his appointment.

(6)   A member of the Electoral and Boundaries Commission may be removed from office only by means of a resolution passed by a two-thirds majority of the members of the Legislative Assembly praying for his or her removal on grounds of incapacity, neglect of duty, or gross misconduct.

(7)   In case of the death, resignation, or removal of any of a member of the Electoral and Boundaries Commission, the vacancy shall be filled as soon as may be practicable in accordance with subsection (1).

(8)   The Electoral and Boundaries Commission may act
        notwithstanding any vacancy in its membership or the
        absence of any member: provided that any decisions of
        the Commission shall require the concurrence of a
        majority of two-thirds of its members.

(9)   Any power or function vested in the Chair of the
        Electoral and Boundaries Commission by this
        Constitution or any law may, if the office of Chair of
        the Commission is vacant or if the holder of that office
        is unable for any reason to perform his or her duties, be
        lawfully exercised by a Deputy Chair elected by the
        Commission from amongst the Commissioners
        appointed under paragraph (a) of subsection (1).

(10)   The Electoral and Boundaries Commission shall
        regulate its own procedure and shall not be subject to
        the direction or control of any other person or authority.

144. Powers and Functions of Electoral and Boundaries Commission

(1)   Subject to this Constitution and in accordance with any
        provisions prescribed by Act of Parliament, the
        Electoral and Boundaries Commission shall have
        responsibility for –
        (a)   supervising the administration of elections and
                referendums at national and local levels of
                government and supervising the conduct of
                election and referendum campaigns, in order to
                ensure that elections and referendums are
                conducted freely, fairly and lawfully;
        (b)   supervising the compilation of electoral rolls and
                facilitating the registration of voters;

(c)   ensuring compliance with such laws as may be in effect to regulate the registration of political parties and campaigns, the nomination of candidates, and donations and expenditures for political purposes;

(d)   the revision of constituency boundaries in accordance with section 145; and

(d)   such other functions, relating to ensuring the free and fair conduct of elections and referendums, as may be vested in the Commission by Act of Parliament.

(2)   In the exercise of its functions under this Constitution or any law the Electoral and Boundaries Commission shall not be subject to the direction or control of any other person or authority.

(3)   The Electoral and Boundaries Commission may, to the extent necessary or reasonable for the fulfilment of its functions, confer powers or impose duties on any local authority and, with the approval of the Permanent Secretary of the department concerned, on any public officer.

145. Delimitation of Constituencies

(1)   The Electoral and Boundaries Commission shall keep under review the constituencies for elections to the Legislative Assembly, including –

(a)   the number of constituencies,

(b)   the names of constituencies,

(c)   the boundaries of constituencies, and

(d)   the total number of members to be returned from constituencies and lists.

(2)   Each constituency for elections to the Legislative
       Assembly shall, as nearly as may be reasonably
       practicable, contain an equal number of registered
       electors; provided, that in determining the boundaries
       of constituencies the Electoral and Boundaries
       Commission may deviate from strict proportionality, by
       no more than +/- 10%, to the extent reasonably
       justifiable so as to give due consideration to –
       (a)   community or diversity of interests,
       (b)   physical features and natural boundaries,
       (c)   historical identity,
       (d)   local government boundaries, and
       (e)   sparsity or density of population.

(3)   The Electoral and Boundaries Commission shall submit
       a report on the revision of constituency boundaries to
       the Legislative Assembly, at intervals of not less than
       every ten years.

(4)   As soon as may be after the Electoral and Boundaries
       Commission has submitted a report under subsection
       (3) of this section, the Prime Minister shall lay before
       the Legislative Assembly a draft Order for giving effect
       to the recommendations contained in the report, and
       that draft Order may also make provision for any
       matters which appear to the Prime Minister to be
       incidental to or consequential upon the other provisions
       of the draft.

(5)   If the motion for the approval of a draft Order is passed
       by a resolution of the Legislative Assembly, the Prime
       Minister shall submit it to the President who shall make
       an Order-in-Council accordingly.

(6)   If the motion for the approval of any draft Order under this section is rejected by the Legislative Assembly, or not passed by the Legislative Assembly within three months, the Prime Minister shall without delay inform the Electoral and Boundaries Commission, and shall invite the Electoral and Boundaries Commission to reconsider its report.

(7)   If after reconsideration of the report in terms of subsection (6) the Electoral and Boundaries Commission submits another report, with or without modifications, the Prime Minister shall lay before the Legislative Assembly a draft Order for giving effect to the recommendations in the second report, and that draft order shall be deemed to have been approved by the Legislative Council after three months have elapsed from the date of its submission, unless during that time the draft Order is rejected by a resolution of the Legislative Assembly passed by a two-thirds majority its members.

(8)   An Order made under this section shall come into force upon the next dissolution of the Legislative Assembly after the Order has been made and shall apply to the general election immediately following that dissolution.

146. Referendums

(1)   Subject to the provisions of this section, Parliament may provide by law for the holding of –
        (a)   'constitutional referendums', to determine whether the people of Northumbria consent to a bill for a constitutional amendment under the terms of subsection (5) of section 147.

(b) 'consultative referendums', to ascertain the views of the people of Northumbria on any proposed bill, other than a bill for the amendment of this Constitution.

(2) No referendum shall be held unless –
   (a) the subject matter of the referendum has been certified as allowable under the terms of this section by Attorney-General; and
   (b) the Electoral and Boundaries Commission has certified before the date of the poll is set that the wording of the question to be put to the people in the referendum is unbiased and unambiguous.

(3) A referendum may not be held on –
   (a) a money bill;
   (b) withdrawal from any treaty;
   (c) any matter within the exclusive competence of the courts; or
   (d) any general question of policy not presented in the form of a bill.

(4) Constitutional referendums binding; and a bill for the amendment of the constitution that has been submitted to a referendum under subsection (5) of section 147 shall not be submitted for presidential assent unless a majority of the votes cast in the referendum are in favour of the bill.

(5) Consultative referendums are merely advisory and shall have no legally binding effect; it is for the Legislative Assembly to decide whether, and how, to give effect to the referendum result.

PART XIII. MISCELLANEOUS PROVISIONS

147. Power to Amend Constitution

(1)   This Constitution may be amended by means of an Act of Parliament enacted in accordance with the provision of this section, and shall not otherwise be amended.

(2)   No Act of Parliament shall be construed as amending this Constitution unless it is stated in the long and short titles of the bill that it is an Act for that purpose.

(3)   A bill for the amendment of this Constitution shall not be deemed to have been passed by the Legislative Assembly unless it has been approved on its final reading by a two-thirds majority of the total number of members of the Legislative Assembly.

(4)   A bill for the amendment of this Constitution that concerns any of the 'entrenched provisions' specified in the Second Schedule shall not be submitted to the President for assent unless it has been approved by a majority of votes cast in a referendum held in accordance with section 146.

(5)   A referendum for the purposes of subsection (4) shall take place on a date to be determined by a resolution of the Legislative Assembly, being a date no later than six months, but no sooner than one month, after the bill has been passed on its final reading by the Legislative Assembly.

(6)   For the purposes of this section an amendment includes
        any alteration, repeal or addition to any part of this
        Constitution, including its preamble and schedules.

(7)   Whenever the Constitution has been amended it shall
        be the duty of the Attorney-General to publish the
        revised consolidated text of the Constitution.

148. Ethical Standards in Public Life

(1)   This section shall apply to –
        (a)   the Prime Minister;
        (b)   Ministers, including the Attorney-General;
        (c)   the Speaker, Deputy Speaker and members of the
                Legislative Assembly;
        (d)   public officers;
        (e)   judges and magistrates;
        (f)   members and officers of local authorities;
        (g)   police officers;
        (h)   members of non-departmental public bodies;
        (i)   the Chair and other members of all Commissions
                established by this Constitution;
        (j)   the Auditor-General and Ombudsman;
        (k)   all other persons in a position of public trust and
                responsibility to whom this section shall be
                applied by law.

(2)   All persons to whom this section applies have a duty to
        conduct themselves in accordance with the following
        principles -
        (a)   Selflessness: holders of public office should act
                solely in terms of the public interest. They should
                not do so in order to gain financial or other

benefits for themselves, their family or their friends;

(b)   Integrity: holders of public office should not place themselves under any financial or other obligation to outside individuals or organisations that might seek to influence them in the performance of their official duties;

(c)   Objectivity: in carrying out public business, including making public appointments, awarding contracts, or recommending individuals for rewards and benefits, holders of public office should make choices on merit;

(d)   Accountability: holders of public office are accountable for their decisions and actions to the public and must submit themselves to whatever scrutiny is appropriate to their office;

(e)   Openness: holders of public office should be as open as possible about all the decisions and actions that they take. They should give reasons for their decisions and restrict information only when the wider public interest clearly demands;

(f)   Honesty: holders of public office have a duty to declare any private interests relating to their public duties and to take steps to resolve any conflicts arising in a way that protects the public interest;

(g)   Leadership: holders of public office should promote and support these principles by leadership and example.

(3)   The Ministerial Code, Standing Orders of the Legislative Assembly, and any Code of Practice adopted by the Public Service Commission, the Judicial Service Commissions, or any other public body, to

guide their disciplinary decisions, shall seek to give effect to these principles.

(4)   There shall be a Committee on Standards in Public Life, which subject to any Act of Parliament shall be organised as an independent non-departmental public body and shall be responsible for –
    (a)   advising on ethical issues relating to standards in public life,
    (b)   conducting broad inquiries into standards of conduct, with a view to making recommendations and improving practice, but without having the authority to conduct investigations into individual allegations of misconduct, and
    (c)   promoting compliance with, and knowledge and awareness of, the seven principles of public life enumerated in subsection (2).

149. Public Honours

(1)   Parliament may provide by law for the creation of noble and chivalric orders in the Republic of Northumbria and for the establishment of civil and military honours, prescribing their hierarchy, grades and eligibility.

(2)   Subject to any conditions prescribed by or under any Act of Parliament enacted in accordance with subsection (1), the President shall award chivalric, civil and military honours on the advice of a Public Honours Committee, which shall consist of –
    (a)   the President, as Chair of the Committee;
    (b)   two Committee members, one of whom shall be a serving or retired senior Public Officer and one

of whom shall be a serving or retired senior officer of the Defence Service, to be appointed by the President on the advice of the Prime Minister, with the concurrence of the Leader of the Opposition;

(c)   two Committee members appointed by the President at his or her own discretion after consultation with such social, cultural or religious organisations, or other civil-society interests, as the President may see fit to consult.

(3)   The members of the Public Honours Committee, other than the Chair, shall serve for renewable terms of three years, unless they resign in writing to the President or are removed on grounds of misbehaviour or for other stated cause by a two-thirds majority of the Legislative Assembly.

(4)   The Public Honours Committee shall ensure that honours are awarded in accordance with the principles of merit, fairness and openness, in recognition of genuine public service and worthy achievements, and not for any party-political or personal consideration.

(5)   A citizen of Northumbria who immediately before the appointed day possessed any title of nobility, whether for life or hereditary, shall not be prevented from using that title, and any citizen of Northumbria who is heir to a hereditary title of nobility shall not be prevented from inheriting and using that title; but no new hereditary peerages shall be created in Northumbria.

(6)   Parliament may make additional provision by law for the organization and functioning of the Public Honours Commission.

150. Presidential Commissions and Public Inquiries

(1)   The President, acting on ministerial advice, may in accordance with this section –
    (a)   establish a Presidential Commission to inquire into and report upon –
        i.   the working of any existing law or policy,
        ii.   the necessity or expediency of any legislation or policy,
        iii.   any other matter of public importance where a question of legislation or policy is to be evaluated; and
    (b)   establish a Public Inquiry to inquire into and report upon –
        i.   the administration of the Government or any department thereof,
        ii.   the conduct of any public officer,
        iii.   any disaster or accident (whether due to natural causes or otherwise) in which members of the public were killed or injured or were or might have been exposed to risk of death or injury, or
        iv.   any other matter of public importance where a question of fact is to be determined.

(2)   The instrument establishing a Presidential Commission or Public Inquiry under subsection (1) shall prescribe –
    (a)   the title of the Presidential Commission or Public Inquiry,
    (b)   the names of the persons nominated its Chairperson and members,

(c)   its terms of reference, any special provisions respecting the manner in which the Presidential Commission or Public Inquiry is to proceed,

(d)   the date for the commencement of its work, and

(e)   the date for delivery of its report.

(3)   The President on ministerial advice may –

      (a)   remove for incapacity, gross misconduct or other stated cause –

          i.   the Chairperson of any Presidential Commission or Public Inquiry,

          ii.   any other member of a Presidential Commission or Public Inquiry;

      (b)   appoint any other person as the Chairperson or as a member of the Presidential Commission or Public Inquiry, whether to fill a vacany arising from the death, resignation or removal of the Chairperson or any member, or otherwise;

      (c)   appoint any other person as an assessor to assist any Presidential Commission or Public Inquiry;

      (d)   alter the terms of reference of a Presidential Commission or Public Inquiry,

      (e)   alter the date of commencement; or

      (f)   alter the date for the delivery of its report.

(4)   An instrument for establishing a Presidential Commission or Public Inquiry under subsection (2) or altering any of the particulars in accordance with subsection (3) shall, before coming into effect –

      (a)   be presented to Parliament by a responsible Minister, and

      (b)   be the subject of a debate on a substantive motion in the Legislative Assembly.

(5) An instrument under paragraph (a)(ii) or (b) to (f) inclusive of subsection (3) shall not be issued except with the concurrence of the Chairperson of the Presidential Commission or Public Inquiry concerned.

(6) A person shall not be appointed as a Chairperson or member of a Presidential Commission or Public Inquiry unless the responsible minister is reasonably satisfied that the person to be appointed –
(a) is suitably qualified and experienced;
(b) has no conflict of interest likely to impair his or her neutrality or independence.

(7) Whenever it is proposed to appoint a public officer as the Chairperson or a member of a Presidential Commission or Public Inquiry, the responsible minister shall consult the Civil Service Commission before nominating that person.

(8) Whenever it is proposed to appoint a serving or retired judge as the Chairperson or a member of a Presidential Commission or Public Inquiry, the responsible minister shall consult the relevant Judicial Service Commission before nominating that person.

(9) A Presidential Commission or Public Inquiry shall have the power to summon any person to appear before it for the purpose of giving evidence or providing information, for which purposes each Presidential Commission or Public Inquiry shall have the power to enforce the attendance of witnesses and examine them on oath, affirmation or otherwise, and to compel the production of documents or other materials or information as required for its proceedings.

(10) Each Presidential Commission and Public Inquiry –
    (a)   shall subject to any rules prescribed by the instrument of its establishment, regulate its own procedure; and
    (b)   shall not be subject to the direction or control of any other person or authority.

(11) A Presidential Commission and Public Inquiry shall, on or before the date prescribed for the delivery of its report, report its findings, and with any recommendations, to the minister responsible, and a copy of the report shall without delay be presented to Parliament.

(12) Further provision relating to the organisation, conduct, powers and duties, and financial arrangements, of Presidential Commissions and Public Inquiries, and for connected purposes, may be made by Act of Parliament.

(13) Until other provision is made under subsection (12), the Public Inquires Act 2005, in so far as it is not incompatible with this section, shall continue to have effect, and the provisions of the Public Inquires Act 2005 shall apply to Presidential Commissions in the same manner and to the same extent as to statutory Public Inquiries.

151. Policing

(1) Parliament shall provide by law for the establishment and regulation of Police Services in Northumbria and for the appointment, qualifications, tenure and salaries and allowances of Police Officers, provided that -

(a)   Chief Constables shall be appointed by the President on the advice of the Prime Minister with the concurrence of the Leader of the Opposition and after consultation with the Public Service Commission; and

(b)   all appointments to any office in any Police Service shall be made in accordance with a Code of Practice to be prescribed by the Public Service Commission under section 125.

(2)   All policing in Northumbria shall be conducted with the minimum of force, in accordance with Sir Robert Peel's 'Nine Principles of Policing'.

152. National Development Authority

(1)   There shall be established a National Development Authority, which shall include –

(a)   the Minister responsible for National Development, being a Minister of Cabinet rank assigned by the Prime Minister, as Chair of the National Development Authority;

(b)   such other Ministers as may be assigned to the National Development Authority by the Prime Minister, which shall include those Ministers having responsibility for finance, the economy, infrastructure, education or social affairs;

(c)   such persons as may from time to time be appointed to the National Development Authority by the President on the advice of the Prime Minister, being persons who in the opinion of the Prime Minister –

(i)   are qualified and experienced in development economics, planning, infrastructural improvements, or social affairs, or related fields of expertise;

(ii)   represent Northumbrian industry, commerce, banking, professional associations, trade unions, or the voluntary sector.

(3)   It shall be the duty of the National Development Authority to –

(a)   produce, at intervals not exceeding five years, an integrated and comprehensive National Development Plan for approval by the Legislative Assembly;

(b)   coordinate Government and non-governmental action towards the implementation of the National Development Plan;

(c)   report annually to the Legislative Assembly on progress towards the implementation of the National Development Plan.

(4)   In the performance of its duties the National Development Authority shall –

(a)   consult with the general public, employers, employees, and other affected interests, at all stages of planning and implementation; and

(b)   have regard to the Duties and Responsibilities of the Republic specified in Part IV of this Constitution, and in particular the need to raise standards of living and eradicate poverty.

(5)   Parliament may make further provision by law for the organization and operation of the National Development Authority.

153. Religion-State Relations

(1)   The Republic honours the foundational historical role of Christianity in Northumbrian society, and values and affirms the continuing contribution of Christian churches and other religious communities to promoting virtue, integrity, peace, mutual solidarity, and the common good.

(2)   Parliament may provide for the disestablishment of the Church of England and for the recognition of an independent Church in Northumbria, by means of an Act of Parliament extending to Northumbria the provisions, *mutatis mutandis,* of the Welsh Church Act 1914.

(3)   Until and unless an Act of Parliament is enacted under subsection (2), the Church of England in Northumbria shall continue to enjoy its existing rights and privileges; provided, that –
   (a)   no Church Measure passed by the General Synod of the Church of England shall have effect as law in Northumbria unless it is approved by the Legislative Assembly and assented to by the President; and
   (b)   any ecclesiastical appointment to any office or benefice formerly within the gift of the Crown shall be made by the President, acting on the advice of such ecclesiastical body as may be prescribed by law.

(4)   Nothing in this Constitution shall invalidate any provision, not unfairly discriminatory against or in favour of any particular religion or denomination, that may be made by or in accordance with law for: the

public funding of religious schools; the employment of chaplains in public institutions; the allocation of public funds to the upkeep of religious buildings of aesthetic, cultural or historical importance; making grants of public money to religious charities; the exemption of religious bodies from certain taxes; the recognition of religious festivals as public holidays; or the restriction of trading and other non-essential activities on religious days of rest.

154. Interpretation

(1)   In this Constitution, unless it is otherwise provided or the context otherwise requires –

(a)   "Act" or "Act of Parliament" means an Act of the Parliament of Northumbria;

(b)   "the appointed day" means the day on which this Constitution comes into force under the provisions of Section 155;

(c)   "Cabinet" means the Cabinet of Northumbria established by section 63;

(d)   "Chief Justice" means the Chief Justice of the Supreme Court of Northumbria;

(e)   "Court of Appeal" means the Court of Appeal of Northumbria;

(f)   "existing law" means any law in force in Northumbria or any part thereof immediately before the appointed day;

(g)   "High Court" means the High Court of Northumbria constituted section 113;

(h)   "judge" means the holder of any judicial office, but does not include a magistrate;

(i)   "law" means any law for the time being in force in Northumbria; and includes this Constitution, any Act of Parliament and any proclamation, regulation, order, by-law or other act of authority made thereunder, the English common law and equity for the time being in so far as they are not excluded by any other law in force in Northumbria, and any custom or usage which has acquired the force of law in Northumbria or any part thereof under the provisions of any Act or under a judgement of a Court of competent jurisdiction.

(j) "Legislative Assembly", or "Assembly", means the Legislative Assembly of Northumbria constituted under the provisions of Section 78;

(k) "Minister" means a Minister of Northumbria holding office under Section 64 includes the Prime Minister and, unless the context otherwise required, the Attorney-General;

(l) "Minister responsible for Finance" means the Finance Minister or any other Minister for the time being having chief responsibility for the management of public finance,

(m) "office of profit" means any office in the service of Northumbria carrying the right to salary, and includes any office declared by Act to be an office of profit;

(n) "Order-in-Council" means an order made by the President on the advice of a responsible Minister;

(o) "Parliament" means the Parliament of Northumbria established under Section 76;

(p) "President" means the President of Northumbria;

(q) "proclamation" means a proclamation made by the President under his or her hand and the Public Seal of Northumbria and published in the Northumbria Gazette;

(r)   "property" includes real and personal property, any estate or interest in any real or personal property, any debt, anything in action, and any other right or interest;

(s)   "public officer" means a member of the Public Service as defined by Section 120;

(t)   "Public Service Commission" means the Public Service Commission of Northumbria established under Section 120;

(u)   "reported donor" means a person who has donated money, goods or services to any political party, candidate, or election or referendum campaign, to or in excess of the amount to be prescribed by Act of Parliament under subsection (3) of section 142, whose donation is reported to the Electoral and Boundaries Commission;

(v)   "salary" includes salary or wages, allowances, superannuation rights, free or subsidised housing, free or subsidised transport, and other privileges capable of being valued in money;

(w)   "Speaker" means the Speaker of the Legislative Assembly, and unless the context otherwise requires, includes the Deputy Speaker when acting on behalf of the Speaker; and

(x)   "Supreme Court" means the Supreme Court of Northumbria established by section 114.

(2) Unless the context otherwise requires, where in this Constitution reference is made to a specified Part, Section or Schedule, that reference shall be construed as a reference to that Part or Section of, or that Schedule to, this Constitution; and, where reference is made to a specified section or paragraph, that reference shall be construed as a reference to that subsection of the Section, or that paragraph of the subsection, in which the reference occurs.

(3) Where under the provisions of this Constitution a person is required to take and subscribe an oath, he or she shall be permitted, if he or she so desires, to comply with that requirement by taking and sub-scribing an equivalent affirmation without religious invocation.

(4) Where in this Constitution reference is made to the functions of any office, that reference shall, unless the context otherwise requires, be construed as a reference to the functions of that office and to any powers and authorities that may lawfully be exercised by, and any duties that may be required to be performed by, the holder of that office.

(5) Where in this Constitution reference is made to any officer by the term designating his or her office, that reference shall, unless the context otherwise requires, be construed as a reference to the officer for the time being lawfully performing the functions of that office.

(6) Where this Constitution confers any power to make any appointment to any office, the person or authority having power to make the appointment shall, unless the context otherwise requires, have power, exercisable in a like manner –

    (a)   to direct that a person other than the person appointed shall, during any period that the person appointed is unable to perform the functions of his or her office owing to absence or inability to act from illness or any other cause, perform the functions of that office;

    (b)   to appoint another person substantively to an office notwithstanding that there is a substantive holder thereof, when that substantive holder is on leave of absence pending relinquishment of his or her office; and

(c)   to direct that a person shall perform the functions of that office when no person has been appointed thereto, either until a contrary direction shall be given by the person or authority having power to make the appointment or until a person shall have been appointed substantively thereto, whichever shall be the earlier.

151. Transitional Provisions

(1)   This Constitution shall be adopted if approved by the Northumbrian Constituent Assembly, by a two-thirds majority of votes cast.

(2)   If this Constitution is approved by a majority of the votes cast in the Northumbria Constituent Assembly, but not by a two-thirds majority, then it shall be put to a referendum, and shall be approved if a majority of the votes cast in the referendum are cast in favour.

(3)   Every person registered to vote for members of the House of Commons in the territory of Northumbria shall be eligible to vote in a referendum held under subsection (2).

(4)   Having been approved in accordance with subsection (1) or subsection (2), this Constitution shall come into effect upon the appointed day, which shall be a day appointed by His Majesty in Council, under the terms of the Northumbria (Independence) Act [DATE].

(5)   The first election to the Legislative Assembly of Northumbria shall take place in accordance with this Constitution within twelve months after the appointed

day; and until such time as those elections are held, the members of the Northumbrian Constituent Assembly shall continue in office as members of a Provisional Legislative Assembly.

(6)   The Provisional Legislative Assembly shall have the same powers, duties, functions and organisation as the Legislative Assembly established by this Constitution, but the provisions relating to the composition, election, qualifications and disqualifications of members, shall not take effect until the first general election under this Constitution has been held.

(7)   The Provisional Legislative Assembly shall proceed without delay to the election of the first President of Northumbria and to the nomination of the first Prime Minister.

(8)   This Constitution shall be directly enforceable as law. From the appointed day, existing law shall, to the extent possible, be interpreted and applied in ways that are compatible with this Constitution; but where there is any incompatibility between this Constitution and any other law, whether enacted before or after the appointed day, this Constitution shall prevail over the incompatible law.

(9)   Subject to the provisions of subsection (8) –
        (a)   the existing English law in force in Northumbria, in so far as it is not inconsistent with this Constitution, shall continue to be in force on and after the appointed day, until repealed or amended in accordance with this Constitution;
        (b)   all rights, obligations and liabilities arising under the existing law shall continue to exist on and

after the appointed day and shall be recognised, exercised and enforced accordingly, and

(c)   proceedings in respect of offences committed against the existing law before the appointed day may be instituted on and after the appointed day in the court having the appropriate jurisdiction, and offenders shall be liable to the punishments provided by the existing law at the time of the offence.

(10)   Where in any existing law reference is made to His Majesty the King in right of the United Kingdom of Great Britain and Northern Ireland, or to the Crown in right of the United Kingdom of Great Britain and Northern Ireland, that reference shall, unless the context otherwise requires, be construed as a reference to the President of Northumbria acting in accordance with this Constitution.

(11)   All property which immediately before the appointed day is vested in His Majesty the King in right of the United Kingdom of Great Britain and Northern Ireland, or to the Crown in right of the United Kingdom of Great Britain and Northern Ireland, or in the Government of the United Kingdom of Great Britain and Northern Ireland, or any Minister or Department thereof, shall, to the extent that such property lies within the jurisdiction of Northumbria, be vested in the Republic of Northumbria, or in the equivalent Minister or Department of the Government of Northumbria.

(12)   The Government of Northumbria shall, for a period of two years after the appointed day, have the authority to make such orders, having the force of law, as may be necessary to bring this Constitution into full operation

and to establish the public institutions required by this Constitution. Such orders may be subsequently repealed or amended in accordance with this Constitution.

(13)   Every person who immediately before the appointed day holds or is acting in any local government, civil service, or judicial office in Northumbria shall, as from the appointed day, hold or act in that office or the corresponding local government, civil service or judicial office established by or under this Constitution as if he or she had been appointed to do so in accordance with the provisions of the Constitution and shall be deemed to have taken any oaths required upon such appointment by any existing law; provided that any person who under the existing law would have been required to vacate office at the expiration of any period or on the attainment of any age shall vacate his or her office under this Constitution upon the expiration of the period or upon the attainment of the age specified by this Constitution, and may be removed in accordance with this Constitution.

(14)   It shall be the duty of the Electoral and Boundaries Commission, before the first election to the Legislative Assembly takes place, to renew the electoral roll and to revise the boundaries of the electoral constituencies in accordance with the provisions of this Constitution.

(15)   For the avoidance of doubt, nothing in this Constitution shall affect the right of any person in Northumbria to inherit a peerage or to use the style and title of a peer, if so entitled, according to existing law and custom.

(16)   The Government of Northumbria shall make provision for the construction or alteration, in or near the City of York, of a suitable Parliament building and an official residence for the President.

(17)   Members of the Armed Forces of the United Kingdom who become citizens of Northumbria on the appointed day shall have the option to transfer, on no less favourable terms of service, to the Northumbrian Defence Service.

(18)   Passports and driving licenses of the United Kingdom shall remain valid in Northumbria until such time as replaced by equivalent Northumbrian documentation.

FIRST SCHEDULE – FORMS OF OATH

1. Oath of Office for the President

I, ..., swear by Almighty God that I will uphold the dignity of the office of President, and will justly and faithfully carry out my duties as President of the Republic of Northumbria in accordance with the Constitution and the law. So help me God.

2. Oath of Office for the Prime Minister and other Ministers

I, ..., being chosen and accepted as Prime Minister [*or:* a Minister] of Northumbria swear by Almighty God that I will to the best of my judgment, at all times when thereto required, freely give my counsel and advice to the President, for the good management of the affairs of Northumbria, and that I will not directly or indirectly reveal such matters as shall be debated in Cabinet and committed to my secrecy, but that I will in all things be a true and faithful Prime Minister [Minister]. So help me God.

3. Oath of Office for the Members of the Legislative Assembly

I, ..., swear by Almighty God that I justly and faithfully carry out my duties as a Member of the Legislative Assembly of Northumbria. So help me God.

4. Judicial Oath

I, ..., swear by Almighty God that I will well and truly serve the Republic of Northumbria in accordance with the Constitution and the law, and I will do right to all manner of people, without fear or favour, affection or ill will. So help me God.

5. Oath of Office for Public Officers and members of Commissions

I, ..., swear by Almighty God that I will well and truly serve the Republic of Northumbria in accordance with the Constitution and the law and will perform my duties with dedication, honesty and integrity, to the best of my ability. So help me God.

6. Oath of Allegiance

I, ..., swear by Almighty God that I will be faithful and bear true allegiance to the Republic of Northumbria. So help me God.

SECOND SCHEDULE – ENTRENCHED PROVISIONS

Section 1 – Foundational Values and Commitments
Section 2 – Supremacy of the Constitution
Sections 7 to 31 inclusive – Fundamental Rights and Liberties
Section 44 – Election of President
Section 46 – Term of Office of President
Section 51 – President to Act on Advice
Section 61 – Executive Power
Section 62 – Cabinet
Section 63 – Appointment of Minister
Section 64 – Removal of Ministers
Section 76 – Parliament
Section 77 – Legislative Authority
Section 78 – Composition of Legislative Assembly
Section 99 – Remuneration of Members
Section 100 – Declaration of Interests
Section 103 – Dissolution of Legislative Assembly
Section 104 – General Elections
Section 106 – Leader of the Opposition
Section 115 – Appointment of Judges
Section 116 – Tenure and Removal of Judges
Section 118 – Judicial Independence and Neutrality
Section 147 – Power to Amend Constitution

"For, brethren, ye have been called unto liberty; only use not liberty for an occasion to the flesh, but by love serve one another. For all the law is fulfilled in one word, even in this; Thou shalt love thy neighbour as thyself."

Galatians 5:13-14

www.ingramcontent.com/pod-product-compliance
Lightning Source LLC
Chambersburg PA
CBHW051348280526
45784CB00007B/2863